DEFIANT
DAUGHTERS

ALSO BY MARCY HEIDISH

FICTION

A Woman Called Moses

The Secret Annie Oakley

Witnesses

Miracles

Deadline

The Torching

NONFICTION

Who Cares? *Simple Ways YOU Can Reach Out*

A Candle At Midnight

Soul and the City

DEFIANT DAUGHTERS

Christian Women of Conscience

MARCY HEIDISH

Liguori
LIGUORI, MISSOURI

Published by Liguori Publications
1 Liguori Drive, Liguori, Missouri 63057
To order, call 800-325-9521 or visit www.liguori.org.

Library of Congress Cataloging-in-Publication Data

Heidish, Marcy.
    Defiant daughters : Christian women of conscience / Marcy Heidish.—1st ed.
        p. cm.
        ISBN 978-0-7648-1950-6
    1. Christian women—Biography. 2. Christian biography. I. Title.
    BR1713.H337 2010
    270.092'2—dc22
    [B]   2010031576

Additional copyright acknowledgments are in Sources and Acknowledgments.

Photo credits: Paul McGuire, xv; Superstock, 3; Wendy Barnes, 6; Granger Collection, 13, 23, 73, 83; Quaker Tapestry Scheme ©, 27; Wikipedia, 33, 63, 86, 120, 153, 163, 206, 210; Library of Congress, 43, 103, 131; myhero.com, 53, 57; Salem Witch Trials Documentary Archive, 85; Sisters of the Presentation of the Blessed Virgin Mary, 93; saintslives. blogspot.com, 113; DavidScottWritings.com, 123; Robert Lentz, 143; Florence Nightingale Museum, 173; Catholic Worker, 183; Maryknoll Sisters, 193; Source unknown, 203, 218; Catholic News Service, 213.

Liguori Publications, a nonprofit corporation, is an apostolate of the Redemptorists. To learn more about the Redemptorists, visit Redemptorists.com.

Cover Design: Dan Forrest-Bank
Cover art: Joan of Arc by Robert Alexander Hillingford / Superstock

Printed in the United States of America
14 13 12 11 10   5 4 3 2 1
First edition

*In Honor of All Unnamed
and Unknown "Defiant Daughters"*

Contents

....

SECTION THREE
DAUGHTERS OF DEDICATION

....

O Lord, I don't want to be a spectator
A tour passenger looking out upon the real world,
An audience to poverty and want and homelessness.

Lord, involve me—call me—
implicate me—commit me—
Lord—help me step off the bus.

~Freda Rajotte

"We keep plugging along here because life is threatened
by other evils worse than death—hatred, vengeance, and
selfishness."

~Ita Ford

For all the saints who went before us
who have spoken to our hearts and touched us with your fire,
we praise you, O God.

For all the saints who lived beside us
whose weaknesses and strengths are woven with our own,
we praise you, O God.

For all the saints who live beyond us
who challenge us to change the world with them,
we praise you, O God.

~Janet Morley

Introduction

Heroines are commanding: "good girls," whose heads are often haloed, or "bad girls," whose heads are often expendable. Spiritual heroines are especially commanding, as they give their all for a world unseen: the flammable field of faith.

Often dismissed or discounted, they take costly stands, make tough choices—and pay the price. Some have names we recognize; many more do not. We crave to know these spiritual trailblazers so that we might, in some way, emulate their courage, their character, and their conscience-driven lives.

What motivates these "defiant daughters," who face many and varied dilemmas? What causes them to surrender security, reputation, comfort and sometimes survival itself—all to answer the call of God and principle? The answers are highly individual, of course, but the portraits on these pages offer clues, conjectures, and some conclusions.

Here is a selection of lives caught in spiritual dilemma, crisis, or conflict. We have much to learn from these passionate women of principle, heirs to the women of the Gospels.

It has always been more difficult for women to break out of conventional expectations and claim their own place in the larger scheme of things. And yet, many did, against long odds. It is notable that such women, in spiritual contexts, have often been seen as mental cases, misfits, menaces, menopausal harpies, or all of the above. Misunderstood or not, they have persevered. In this book, specific spiritual lives are examined for their "tipping points": a question of conscience is faced, weighed, and decided. "Every life includes pivotal moments, roads taken or not," writes Bill Shore. "...Quiet, often solitary acts of conscience have echoes louder than the original sound."

Such choices are exemplified by the cross itself, the center of Christian faith for two thousand years. Women were faithful followers of Jesus, all the way to Calvary and beyond. Women discovered the empty tomb of the resurrection. Women, as apostles, deacons, and converts, turned their homes into the earliest Christian churches, even during times of severe persecution by the state.

The Christian tradition, then, is deeply enriched by those "defiant daughters" who lived the Gospel to a radical, risk-taking degree. In the words of Ita Ford, a Maryknoll sister martyred in El Salvador, "We keep plugging along here, because life is threatened by other evils worse than death—hatred, vengeance, and selfishness." This sentiment is expressed in word and deed by a variety of figures in this book.

Defiant Daughters is divided into three categories, which may overlap in some cases. Here is a mix of mystics and martyrs, reformers and rebels, protectors and preachers. Many live in solidarity with the poor and the oppressed. Some give up lives of comfort for a sense of calling; others bear burdens rather than betray comrades. They are Catholic, Protestant, Quaker, and Orthodox. Whatever their differences, they are all in close communion with God—and they all face some sort of spiritual dilemma.

The "dilemma factor" has been this book's guiding criterion. It is inevitable that many figures could not be included within this book's scope. Among them are medieval laywomen called "Beguines," Scottish Covenanters, notable abbesses such as Hildegard of Bingen, remarkable missionaries such as Gladys Aylward and Amy Carmichael, and certain canonized saints, such as Catherine of Siena. They are numerous, as well as awe-inspiring, these "defiant daughters" of many countries, many cultures, and all races.

The prologue presents a keynote figure, Laura Lopez of Guazapa, whose cry of *"adelante!"* ("forward") expresses the passing of a spiritual torch through conscientious choice. The epilogue brings us into the present with Immaculée Ilibagiza of Rwanda, who made a different kind of choice, which she continues to live out. Between these two women are many others.

Their lives range over one thousand eight hundred years and some ten nations. Those classed as "daring" tend to rebel against existing constraints or put themselves in harm's way. Women categorized as "determined" stand fast, whether that means refusal to inform on friends or give way to adversaries. Heroines in the "dedication" section are strongly motivated by love of God and the oppressed. As noted, there is some fluidity among the classifications. Corrie ten Boom exemplifies this: she is determined, indeed, but extraordinary in her daring to forgive her oppressors. In each case, it is the dominant note that determines the placement.

The stories of these women need not be read in order of appearance. It might be helpful to read the profiles in community with others, for discussion or educational purposes. What would we have done in similar situations? How far would we go for a principle? When does a stand for conscience cost too much? In most cases, there are no easy answers—but there are questions following each chapter to spark conversation and reflection. My source material and ideas for further reading are cited in a list of sources and acknowledgments at the book's conclusion.

However the book is used, it is hoped that these profiles will draw on inspiration from the past to give us inspiration for today and tomorrow.

PROLOGUE
Laura Lopez of Guazapa
(1950-1985)

The knapsack was her only insignia. Always with her, the sack held bread, a Bible, a missal, and a notebook. Laura Lopez wore no habit, no clerical collar, no miter nor maniple. Even so, as she moved through the sloping community of Guazapa, El Salvador, she was warmly greeted by the people she had served since 1979. Six years later, as army bullets struck her down, Laura Lopez passed her knapsack on, shouting her last charge: *"Adelante!*—Forward!"* During her country's devastating civil conflict, Laura had felt called to minister to the peasants living on the side of a dormant volcano.

Guazapa was an endangered community suspected of harboring insurgents against the ruling dictatorship. Ordained clergy did not go to Guazapa or to many villages in the countryside. These were war zones; the risk of death was too great. Priests and nuns were often targeted as those who aided "subversives." Whatever the risks, Laura Lopez made a quiet and lasting decision to follow God's call to minister to the poor. "Whatever you did for one of these least brothers of mine, you did for me," is the radical statement of Jesus Christ from Matthew 25.

Laura Lopez and her husband made a fateful decision—no doubt, the toughest and most costly one of their lives. When they sold their house and moved their family into the war zone of Guazapa, they knew they were putting themselves in harm's way for the sake of the Gospel.

Two years later, when her husband was killed, Laura must have revisited her decision, if only briefly. By then, she and her children were deeply engaged with the people of their new community. And later, as air strikes intensified El Salvador's civil war, Laura again committed herself to stay in Guazapa. She saw it as the way of the cross, and the way of love. This spiritual stance sustained her throughout the years of strife and sacrifice, and through her, it sustained others.

In 1980, after Laura Lopez arrived in Guazapa, Archbishop Oscar Romero was shot dead at the altar while he said Mass. Romero had been an outspoken advocate of the poor and the development of a "new people of God." Laura Lopez, driven by conscience and compassion, felt compelled to be one of those. She was inspired by Rutilio Grande, a Jesuit priest who had gone to live with the peasants of El Salvador in 1970. Grande, assassinated seven years later, organized the poor into small "base communities" that met regularly to reflect on the Scriptures, to pray, and to discuss ways of transforming oppression.

Despite Grande's death, his ideas were passed along, just as Laura's knapsack was handed on almost a decade later.

By the time Laura Lopez moved to Guazapa, there were about fifteen thousand lay catechists and pastoral workers in the field—and in harm's way. The message these pastoral teams carried was threefold: The poor are important to God. The suffering of the poor is not God's will. God is with the weak, the powerless, the indigent.

This was the message carried by the pastoral ministry of Sister Ana, who felt called to help the peasants suffering through El Salvador's civil war. Ana's community elected Laura Lopez as a "Delegate of the Word," a high honor. In the absence of ordained clergy in rural areas, delegates functioned as did the deacons of the early Church, providing spiritual leadership in many situations, except at weddings and official celebrations of the holy Eucharist.

The mission of Laura Lopez was something like that of a circuit-riding minister. In undertaking this office, Laura Lopez was defying life-threatening danger. She was also defying centuries of tradition about women's roles in spiritual leadership positions. She had the courage to live out the promptings of her conscience and her faith—at considerable cost.

Laura Lopez did not go alone to live in Guazapa. She and her husband moved into the war zone with their five children. Laura's husband was fully supportive of the move, as were her children. The children understood their parents' dedication and became committed to their new life. Their oldest son told Laura that he wanted to stay on, even if she left; her initial commitment was for three years.

Sadly, two years after their arrival, Laura's husband was killed in a land-mine explosion and Laura was left to carry on their mission alone. Even after his father's death, her son remained determined to stay in Guazapa. Laura's oldest daughter was also committed to her mother's pastoral ministry.

Even so, one must wonder about the effect of Laura's mission on her children's safety. How did she reconcile her calling to the poor with the calling of motherhood? Did she fear for her children's lives? Or did she fear something more: a lack of spiritual purpose in those young lives? Or worse—a reversal of the values she believed in with all her being.

One thing we do know: Laura could not leave her family with relatives—her siblings had vowed to kill their own sister. Her own brothers had turned in the opposite direction, joining the government's "death squads" and vowing to "eradicate" any suspected "subversives." Perhaps Laura believed that her children were safer with her, under these circumstances. Certainly she wanted to keep the family together. There was little safety anywhere in El Salvador from 1979 to 1985, the duration of Laura's ministry.

Finally, the clearest answer to her dilemma may be the way she lived out her own words to her children: "If we love, we must show it," recorded in the book, *The Hour of the Poor, the Hour of Women: Salvadoran Women Speak,* by Renny Golden. Laura Lopez and her family embodied that credo.

Walking to the region's various villages, Laura visited each community in the pastoral tradition of Saint Paul. She came to be called "the bishop" by Guazapa's people. Renny Golden wrote, "They called her 'the bishop' because she was all they had." Laura ministered to these communities with Sabbath services under the trees and in villagers' homes. Laura went to the people themselves, as needed, for a variety of spiritual and pastoral concerns.

Later, a peasant farmer of Guazapa recalled of Laura: "She once told us that the Good Shepherd never deserted the sheep and she would stay on in Guazapa preaching the Gospel even if only one person remained."

She was true to her word—and her "pastorate" knew it. Perhaps, as a girl of eighteen or so, Laura had heard the radio address of Pope Paul VI. Issued in Bogota, Columbia, in 1968, the speech issued a challenge that made many uncomfortable at the time—and continues to do so to this day: "What can I say to you, men of the ruling class?" the pope had queried his listeners. "What is required of you is generosity. This means the ability to detach yourselves from the stability of your position, which is a position of privilege, in order to serve those who need your worth, your culture, your authority.... Your ears and heart must be sensitive to the voices crying out for bread, concern, justice, and a more active participation in the direction of society." This challenge would have made a deep impression on the young Laura Lopez. And a dozen years later, she was living out her response to that very challenge.

It is inconceivable that Laura Lopez did not recognize the grave risks of such a life. In 1980, she was at work in El Salvador when three American nuns were murdered there, also while working with the poor. (One of those nuns, Sister Ita Ford, is profiled later in this book.) "We keep plugging along here," Ita Ford wrote, "*because life is threatened by evils other than death—vengeance, greed, selfishness* (italics mine)."

Perhaps these words help us to locate another clue to Laura's motivation. Lopez, an indigenous Salvadoran, would have endorsed this statement made by an "outsider" who was drawn to be an "insider." Laura might not live to see great change; her children would. "A prophetic people realize that their gift is for the future of the people," Archbishop Romero believed. "Perhaps the gift we have given to the world is that it is possible to make something new." Laura Lopez wanted to be a part of that re-creation. Her actions indicate her desire for her children to be a part of "the new people of God" (in Romero's words) as well.

Laura's commitment to her conscience and her faith were tested by fire in 1985. In that year, the military government launched its air attack on those they had targeted as "rebels" or as traitorous guerrillas. The authorities were convinced that the poor were Communist insurgents, threatening the stability and survival of the ruling *junta*.

Following this line of thinking, the military bombed them, either as activists or as those who harbored and hid such activists. This translated into the slaughter of thousands of civilians, including women, children, and elderly people.

Lopez, true to her conscience, went into action. With her camera and tape recorder, she documented the invasion of the defenseless people of the countryside. Her letters went out to the Red Cross, to the press, and to a variety of church groups in the United States and elsewhere. Not only were acres of crop-yielding fields destroyed, innocent lives were lost every day.

Lopez sent three of her children out of the war zone. She remained with her oldest son and daughter. As Guazapa's spiritual leader, Laura Lopez felt compelled to "accompany" her people—and to warn against hatred and revenge. "We should not place our faith strictly in weapons," she said, "thinking that the gun is God and that the gun will give us liberty and justice."

Six weeks before her death, Lopez crouched with other villagers in a crude air-raid shelter. Overhead, military aircraft flew low, letting their bombs fall on fields ready for spring planting. Laura was calm—and defiant.

"All of us are hidden in a bomb shelter because we are well aware that their bullets are waiting for us," she wrote. "At this moment, one A-37 is in our vicinity. We are on the shore of the lake.... Meanwhile another plane is bombing Cinquera. We are trying to defend lives, though we can no longer defend our huts or our belongings." Lopez ended her letter on a particularly defiant note.

"God doesn't want it to be that way. They want to terrorize us, but we will not be swayed."

Lopez inspired her people to hold firm, even as they dodged the bombs. These were poor farmers, she noted, watching the destruction of all they had—their land and its fertility. Their children ran screaming to shelters, hiding from the military, whose mission was to "sanitize" the area.

Food ran low. Wounds festered. Thirst worsened. Author Renny Golden reports that "Laura's ability to calm her people even in the midst of crises is still well-remembered." Golden's insightful account of the Lopez ministry shows a leader who was not easily shaken. Lopez was also a practical leader. She knew Guazapa could not hold out much longer.

When the area's commanding general announced a ninety-day bombing campaign, Laura felt compelled to act. Somehow, she had to get to San Salvador. She could not stand by while her people suffered; she wanted to plead Guazapa's cause with the Archdiocese itself. The situation was urgent. With a few companions, she walked most of the way to the capital city and made known the villagers' plight. Even if their lives were saved—what then? Houses, crops, livestock, arable land—everything that supported the community was damaged or destroyed. Massive aid would be needed.

"The martyr's cross has been placed on our shoulders," Laura preached at a Sunday service. "Our people have decided to go this way of the cross, but the final triumph is still down the line. We are Christians and we know what we have to do. But first, we must sacrifice and make a serious decision to do so." And then she spoke a memorable and disturbing sentence. "The first to die are always those with faith."

It was Lent 1985 when Lopez spoke the message of the cross, played out in Guazapa itself. Even so, on Palm Sunday, Lopez led her community to think beyond horror to hope. "We have gotten used to hating, to being afraid," she preached that day. "We have to put an end to that. We have to confront ourselves to kill the false pride within our soul so that a new person may arise, so that a new civilization may come into being—one composed of love." It was the beginning of Holy Week. It was the beginning of the Easter event. It was a brief moment of triumph, commemorated in the liturgy, and in the village, and in the life of Laura Lopez.

Did she sense that her time was running out? Perhaps it was inevitable that she would discern this. Earlier in the month, Lopez had called a meeting of Guazapa's pastoral workers and team members. Her message to them was one of encouragement…and a look toward the future. "Despite fatigue, after making an escape from an invading army, we give thanks to God for protecting us. The work of the base communities must continue, because it if were otherwise, what would become of us?"

Even if she were not there, Laura seemed to say, the ministry must go on. Her words would take on a deeper meaning in hindsight. On April 22, 1985, when another wave of invasion overwhelmed the Guazapa region, Laura Lopez offered reassurance to her people. She would stay with them, she promised. "We can't take off and leave the people here," she told other pastoral workers. "We have already offered our lives for them."

Laura was ready. Her mind and spirit were prepared. Her words indicate no doubt or fear—only resolution. She had come to the same conclusion that Ita Ford had voiced four years earlier in a different part of the country. "There are worse things than death…." That day, Laura could hear the incessant shelling from the government troops. It grew louder; it grew nearer.

Finally, Laura and her oldest daughter decided to make a run for a shelter. Once they reached it, they discovered that it was full to overflowing; there was no room for them inside. Laura and her daughter ran for hiding in the nearby cane fields, trying to escape the ground patrols and hide amongst the stalks still standing.

They were moving so fast, with such energy, Laura Lopez was unaware of the first shot's impact. Her thirteen-year-old daughter remembers how quickly it all happened: "I was running along, just about at my mother's side, when she was hit by a bullet in the back. I said, 'Mama, they've hit you!' Perhaps she hadn't felt it just yet because she kept on running. Then another bullet hit her....She couldn't run anymore....She gave me the knapsack and told me to go forward." The badge of "the bishop" had been passed on. The daughter had heard her mother's last command: *"Adelante!"* The woman fell; the girl survived.

Renny Golden writes, "This final moment symbolizes the church of the poor in which the only promise is that—if you fall—someone else will take your place. The knapsack is handed over. It is a symbol of that church which is bloodstained and passes on a pastor's contraband, passes on the spirit of the one who died." Laura's daughter began to live this out immediately as she hid in the long grasses near her mother's body.

From that vantage point, she saw the shooting of a six-year-old boy from Guazapa. He, too, had been running for refuge amid the cane stalks. He was wounded, bleeding heavily, but not yet dead. With her own socks, Laura's daughter made a bandage for his wound, stopped the bleeding and, under cover of darkness, she carried him to safety through the cane fields. His life was saved. Her mother's was clearly lost. Days later, when the attack ended, Laura's body was located by her daughter and a party of villagers.

In a shed, an informal memorial service was held for Laura. There were wildflowers and lit candles. Laura's photograph was tacked to one wall. As her pastoral team gathered, the people spoke of her

in simple words. She belonged to them, they said. As a follower of
Jesus, she had performed the ultimate loving act he identified—she
had given her life for her friends.

The story of Laura Lopez is not well-known in the wider world.
In El Salvador, however, its message of conscience and courage has
inspired many others.

Laura stands in a long line of "Defiant Daughters" who risked
body and soul for their beliefs. They made costly choices without ceremony or celebration. Some are the subject of story and song; some
stood for God in obscurity. They all reached a decision point that
reversed the usual standards for spiritual women in the world. And
so they live on: a great cloud of witnesses to awe and encourage us.

We will trace some of these distinguished lives which preceded
Laura Lopez and which inspire us to take up her charge: *"Adelante."*

....

Questions for Reflection and Discussion

1. How would you define Laura Lopez's example?
2. What sustained her more than anything?
3. Was she out to prove herself—or do you think she had a
   genuine calling?
4. Why do you think Laura went into Guazapa's war zone?
5. Do you believe Laura was right to function as a pastor?
6. Do you think Laura was selfish regarding the children
   she left behind?
7. What can Laura's life teach us about the cost of conscience?
8. Do we need Laura's kind of commitment today?
9. Would you have gone to minister in Guazapa,
   knowing the risks?
10. Where is "the moment of truth" for this heroine?

SECTION ONE

Daughters of Daring

For all the saints who went before us
who have spoken to our hearts
and touched us with your fire,
we praise you, O God.

Joan of Arc
of Domremy la Pucelle
1412-1431

Her story begins in rippling fields and ends in rippling flames. In the short span of time between those markers, one of Europe's most famous heroines took a costly stand for conscience and followed a divine call across an international stage. She has been demonized, canonized, analyzed, psychologized, reconstructed, deconstructed, dramatized, and rhapsodized.

And yet, when one looks behind the icon, the story of Joan of Arc still stands, simple and stunning, as a template for God's defiant daughters. Legend predicted that a French virgin would arise from Lorraine to deliver her nation from foreign oppression. On the Feast of the Epiphany, January 6, 1412, heavenly signs were said to mark the birth of a special child. This child took the form of a peasant's daughter, born to an unlettered farming family in the French province of Lorraine.

It was an unremarkable beginning for a girl who would one day lead an army, rally a country, and catalyze the conclusion of the Hundred Years War. Her commander was not her father, to whom she owed obedience, nor was it even the king she helped to crown. "I was born for this," she said later. "It is God's will to deliver the people of France."

As a child, Joan helped her siblings work her parents' farm and became adept at spinning. Much later, contemporaries remember her as a normal, obedient, sweet-spirited girl who only evidenced upset when the bell-ringer forgot his duties at the church. The bells were important to Joan; for her, they signaled times of prayer, wherever she was, even in the fields.

And then her prayer times changed forever. "When I was thirteen I had a voice from God....The first time I was terrified. The voice came to me about noon; it was summer in my father's garden....There was a great light all about." Later, she attested to other light-drenched visions in which she sometimes saw Saints Michael, Catherine, and Margaret. "I saw them with my own eyes as well as I see you," she later attested. Fearing ridicule, however, Joan kept these experiences secret for three years.

Mystical revelations were dangerous in the 1400s. If not sanctioned by the Church, such revelations could be signs of converse with the Evil One. Today, we would tend to interpret such experiences as evidence of psychosis, but in Joan's case there is no evidence of any mental imbalance. To her, mystical revelation was a gift she guarded—until her sixteenth year.

Then something critical happened. Joan's voices changed their message. Initially they had simply urged her to be good and pious. However, in 1428 the revelations began urging her to go into action. God wished her to relieve the suffering of the French people. Joan had come to one of two watershed moments in her life, where she had to make hard and costly choices. Stay as she was? Or risk all to follow God's call?

She later said she would prefer to stay home and spin wool with her mother, "but since God commanded me to go, I must do it." And so, at sixteen, she made a life-changing decision. She stepped out in faith to fulfill the divine mission she had been given: to free France from British oppression and to crown the heir apparent, the Dauphin Charles de Ponthieu. France had long been weakened by foreign occupation—only with a crowned king could it reclaim its autonomy, strength, and dignity.

Joan was not a political person, and yet she was shrewd and sagacious. She never contradicted herself, and everything she did was motivated by her sense of divine calling. Her unwavering obedience to God, however, set her at odds with all the expectations and traditions of women in her day—and a high price accompanied such disobedience.

It began with her disappearance from her father's house. Without a word, she ran away from home and put on men's clothes—a sensible move to keep herself safe from men's advances. Through a series of connections and personal conviction, Joan rode more than three hundred miles in winter to seek an audience with the dauphin at Chinon. Losing power every day, his demoralized army in disarray, Charles was at a low ebb. Joan's appearance must have seemed an answer to prayer. Although she had never seen the dauphin before, Joan picked him out from a room of glittering nobles. Shining with unshakable conviction, she brought glad tidings indeed: It was God's will that the dauphin be king, and she would make it happen. Here was a divine messenger—just for Charles.

"The Maid," as Joan called herself, must have been a highly charismatic person, able to persuade Charles of her calling. He did have her investigated—and then to the amazement of historians ever after, Charles granted Joan the leadership of his faltering army. Striking an oddly prescient note, Joan told him that she would only last a year and there was much work to be done.

Joan of Arc's journey included these cities.

In the meantime, she became a kind of icon, embodying her people's hopes for freedom against overwhelming odds. With her feminine face and her masculine clothing, she seemed to unite the disparate images of the Virgin Mary and the Archangel Michael. Her divine calling enhanced the prophecy that preceded her, infusing hope in the deeply religious soldiers. In addition, Joan seemed to possess certain powers that are unexplained by science or psychology.

She foresaw her future wounding and capture. She also predicted the final routing of the British from French soil. Further she requested a sword hidden under the altar of a church she had never visited; the sword was there. It is impossible to say how much her precognition enhanced her standing with her troops; many of her predictions did not come true until after her death. In any case, the soldiers felt her personal warmth and support.

In gleaming armor, astride a white horse, she was a unique savior. Raising the French standard, she rallied the troops and led her first charge—"For God and for France!" In addition to her strong faith and her personal charisma, Joan turned out to be a fine military strategist; far more than a standard-bearer.

She took a more aggressive approach than previous commanders and focused her attention on Orléans: the war's key city, the gateway to southern France—under siege for seven months. For the French, the loss of Orléans seemed imminent, but Joan, undeterred, led the army to this strategic location.

During this intense battle, Joan was shot in the shoulder with an arrow. After a brief retreat, she pulled the arrow out herself. Soon thereafter, to the troops' amazement, she returned to the field. Morale rose. The French won the day. The siege was lifted; church bells rang out. In joy and triumph, Joan was hailed as "The Maid of Orléans." A series of other victories at Patay and other towns increased French morale and cleared the path for the dauphin's coronation. On July 17, 1429, Joan's efforts finally led to this historic event: The dauphin was crowned as King Charles VII in Rheims Cathedral, amid solemnity and ceremony.

Now a national hero, Joan had fulfilled the mission she had discerned from her revelations. She also became a prime target for the enemy, especially the traitorous Burgundians. From a distance, they watched her, awaiting their chance to seize her.

The army's morale was inextricably linked to Joan's presence. If Joan could be removed from the equation, the French might lose their momentum. Indeed, Charles delayed and equivocated, causing a defeat at Paris. As the king lost confidence in "The Maid," the enemy closed in. During the battle for Compiegne, Joan's party was routed and, as commander, she joined the rear guard—the last officer to leave the field.

In this position she was vulnerable, and the Burgundians ambushed her, forcing her from her horse and taking her captive. In turn, the Burgundians sold their "prize" to the enemy—the English. Naturally, this turn of events was a tremendous blow to the French forces. However, King Charles and his advisors lacked the courage and strength to manage a rescue. Joan of Arc, so recently the heroine of France, was abruptly abandoned to face the formidable power of church and state—alone. Here begins the second and final chapter in Joan's "profile in courage." Her ultimate watershed moment lay just ahead.

In an attempt to break her spirit, Joan's captors questioned her relentlessly, day and night. When she was forced to wear women's clothes, she was nearly raped by her guards. Against orders, she reverted to male garb, though this was illegal at the time and considered unscriptural as well.

Her year-long inquisition became a form of torture, designed to wear her down. The trial, of course, was rigged, prearranged by the Burgundian, Pierre Cauchon, the bishop of Beauvais and close collaborator with the British.

The great surprise of Joan's "trial" was Joan herself. No one had bargained on a quick-thinking, sharp-tongued, intelligent, and lucid "defendant." Before the interrogation process wore her down, she gave many answers that showed a fine weave of wit and faith. In the face of such overwhelming adversaries, she chose the demeanor of defiance and remained true to God and her beliefs. "On being asked whether she did not believe that she was subject to the church which is on earth...she replied, 'Yes, but our Lord must be served first.'"

A "trick question" was posed to her. Was she in a state of grace? If she answered "no," she would damn herself; if she answered "yes," she would speak as a heretic, since no one knew the mind of God. Well? Was she in a state of grace? "If I am not, may God place me there," she retorted. "If I am, may God keep me there. But if I were in a state of sin, do you think the Voice would come to me?"

Her interrogators were unable to refute that—but they had many more questions for Joan, most of them touching on the subject of her "voices." She was asked what dialects her "voices" spoke. "A better one than yours," she shot back. The next question was presented. Did Saint Margaret speak English? "Why would she speak English," Joan demanded, "since she wasn't on the English side?"

"The Maid of Orléans" still faced the most dangerous charges: heresy and witchcraft. Convictions for witchcraft and heresy resulted in the same penalty: death at the stake—by fire.

In the end, the truth really didn't matter to Joan's inquisitors. All that mattered was her condemnation. She must be removed as the enemy's standard-bearer, its inspiration, its icon. The images she combined were too potent: crusader, hero, damsel, virgin queen.

Perhaps her judges did believe that something strange and otherworldly was at work in Joan of Arc. After all, how could an illiterate peasant girl—on her own—possess such effective skills in leadership, military tactics, and courtroom defense?

Over and over again, the investigation came back to Joan's mysticism. She adhered to her belief in her "voices" with a steadfastness that baffled the "court." When cautioned to tell the truth, Joan responded with a piercing dart of folk wisdom: "Children say that people are hung sometimes for speaking the truth," she retorted.

It was suggested that Joan was flouting the commandment to honor one's father and mother. "Since God commanded [my mission], even if I had a hundred fathers and mothers, even if I had been a king's daughter, I would have done it...I would rather die than do anything I thought was a sin against the will of God." This additional statement is attributed to Joan by a later source. "One life is all we have, and we live it as we believe in living it. But to sacrifice what you are, and to live without belief, that is a fate more terrible that dying."

After months of intense grilling, however, nineteen-year-old Joan began to give way. Deprived of sleep, kept in isolation, menaced by the guards, and constantly questioned, she became desolate, confused, and exhausted. Taking advantage of her state, Cauchon led her outside the prison walls and showed her the platform with the stake already in place.

Wood was piled high around it. Cauchon encouraged Joan to look long at this instrument of execution. Did she really want to burn to death in the marketplace? Amid an apparent "dark night of the soul," Joan seems to have temporarily lost touch with her guiding "voices." She was presented with a document of several pages, which she was unable to read. In weariness and desperation, she signed it with the halting letters of one learning how to write: "JEHANNE."

Now "The Maid" would not burn—but she would be imprisoned for life. The French troops would hear that she gave way. The impact on their morale would be serious. Joan must have entertained such thoughts as she reflected on her choice. Three days passed. And during that time Joan made the hardest decision of her life. Perhaps her own words came back to her, "I would rather die than do anything I thought was a sin against the will of God."

The three days were up. Joan of Arc summoned her tormentors one last time. Her "voices," she said, told her that God was grieved by her recent renunciation of her beliefs. And then, before her captors and judges, she denied her earlier confession; she could not betray her conscience.

This was her ultimate watershed moment—the ultimate choice. She elected to die for her beliefs, even if that meant the label of "heretic" and "witch." In the end, she was true to her conscience. Ironically, the actual "crime" that sealed her fate was the wearing of men's clothes by a woman.

Ten thousand people turned out to watch the "Maid of Orléans" burn at the stake in the marketplace of Rouen. Before her execution, Joan's head was shaved and she was forced to wear a penitent's plain shift. A tall pointed cap, inscribed with her "crimes" and "sins," was placed on her head. She was then paraded through the marketplace to mount the platform. She asked if she might have a cross to hold. Her request was denied. She asked if someone might hold a cross at eye-level. This request was also denied.

One wonders what sustained Joan through her final hours and, especially, those final moments. If she felt abandoned by God, she gave no sign of it. She knew well that Jesus had suffered agony on the cross; perhaps she felt she shared his passion. It is impossible to ascertain her thoughts at that time, but Christ was clearly on her mind. As the fire was kindled and her shift took flame, she called on the name of Jesus several times. It is said that she clasped a crude cross made of twigs for her by a compassionate bystander.

Canny to the end, Cauchon, the bishop of Beauvais, ordered the fire to be extinguished when he assumed Joan was dead. Her charred body was exhibited to the crowd so that no one could suggest she had experienced a mystical deliverance. When all had viewed Joan's remains, the fire was rekindled until her body was reduced to ashes. These were thrown into the Seine so that nothing would be left. (Today, a statue of Joan stands on the place where she burned to death in Rouen's marketplace.)

Over a decade later, Church authorities opened an inquest into Joan's condemnation. The clergy carefully examined the transcripts of her trial and previous interrogations. The verdict was unanimous: *Innocent.*

More than a decade after that inquest, British forces were expelled from the city of Rouen, and twenty-two years after Joan's death the British left French soil forever, thus ending the Hundred Years War. Even so, Joan was not officially recognized by her Church until 1920. She may be the only person both condemned (as a heretic) and canonized (as a saint) by the same religious body.

Even before her official recognition, Joan of Arc was venerated as one of the patron saints of France, as she still is today. In many ways, Joan was like the "little ones," the common folk, the people who had followed Jesus of Nazareth and trusted him. This was the faith of Joan, who trusted her divine connection and, in the end, who did not abandon her conscience, her God, or her calling.

Questions for Reflection and Discussion

1. How would you characterize Joan of Arc's life?
2. What sustained her more than anything?
3. Was she motivated by faith—or rebellion?
   Could she have been motivated by both?
4. How did Joan's mysticism motivate her?
5. Was Joan of Arc's "mission" egocentric or heroic?
6. Do you think she was trying to be a "star"—
   or a true servant of God?
7. What can Joan's life teach us in our time?
8. Where do we need Joan of Arc's daring faith today?
9. Would you have given your life for a belief such as hers?
10. Where is "the moment of truth" for this heroine?

Anne Hutchinson of Boston
1591–1643

The trial of Anne Hutchinson

In her own day some called her a saint. Some went so far as to call her a "Satan" and a "New England Jezebel." Today, however, she is hailed as a pioneer of American religious liberty. In a belated tribute, a statue of her, cast in bronze, stands before the Statehouse of Massachusetts, overlooking historic Boston Common.

Who was the controversial woman depicted in the statue? Why did she have to pay so dearly for her religious convictions? Anne Hutchinson, a Puritan convert, was first and foremost, the devoted matriarch of a huge family. In addition, she became Boston's beloved midwife—and a unique, unofficial lay minister to the town's women. Soon after she began holding meetings for them, men were also drawn to the Hutchinsons' commodious home.

Directly across the street, Governor John Winthrop kept a wary eye on these unsanctioned gatherings—and on their charismatic hostess, whom he grudgingly dubbed "a masterpiece of woman's wit." At first, he could do little more than observe. After all, Anne's husband was one of the most prosperous and prominent newcomers to Boston in 1634.

I like to think of Anne Hutchinson on those evenings when her home shone with light and brimmed with hospitality. Hanging from the great room's ceiling, the long candle-bar would cast an amber glow across the benches set out for the Hutchinsons' guests. The talk in this house was illuminating as well. Here, ideas about spirituality and Scripture could be freely exchanged.

Anne, the daughter of an English minister, was well-educated and knowledgeable about biblical studies. Somehow, through thirteen pregnancies, she had maintained her life of devotional prayer and study. Certainly, this was a rare set of roles for a woman of Anne's era. Perhaps it irritated Winthrop that she managed them all so well.

At her large house on School Street, all were welcome. Winthrop would have noticed the profusion of lanterns bobbing toward the Hutchinson home. There, Anne encouraged extemporaneous prayer, Bible study, and discussion of Sunday sermons.

Boston's women blessed Mistress Hutchinson for these evenings; many goodwives could not attend Sabbath meetings due to child-bearing and child rearing. Recent emigrants, they sought spiritual guidance for their life in this raw new town so far from home. Anne Hutchinson, an emigrant herself, addressed their special spiritual needs.

Even the "common people," unchurched laborers, loved her. She had a way of communicating even the most complex theology. It was perhaps unfortunate that one such worker's enthusiasm was overheard.

"If you'd go along with me tonight," he told a comrade, "I'll bring you to a woman that teaches better Gospel than any of your black-coats at a university, a woman of another spirit entirely...." However, the ministers and magistrates remained suspicious.

They remembered a delay in Anne's acceptance by Boston Church over a doctrinal disagreement—a small point, soon resolved, but the clergy had not forgotten. They would wait. They would watch. They would listen for any sign of unorthodoxy from this popular Mistress Hutchinson and sent spies into her meetings.

It is impossible to underestimate the power of these men. The Massachusetts Bay Colony was not chartered as a bastion of religious tolerance. Instead, the colony was formed as a new "Promised Land" for the Puritan elect and elite. Boston was to be a "city on a hill" where its sober values were strictly enforced. Any deviation from the norm would, and did, invite harsh punishment.

For speaking publicly against the ministers, one Phillip Ratcliffe was fined, whipped, and banished, after both his ears were cut off. Two other dissenters were censured by the courts and sentenced to stand in public with their tongues held in cleft sticks. Such personal examples made no small impact on Boston's citizens.

Anne Hutchinson would have heard about these incidents. Even so, she insisted on her right to speak in private, in her own home, and merely raised matters of interpretation. When Anne could not see a text as a minister did, she was not afraid of open discussion or commentary. Her theology had a more liberal cast than was common in Boston. Anne emphasized God's mercy and grace rather than inexhaustible divine wrath. An excessive fear of damnation plagued many of the women and this, too, grieved Anne.

Perhaps as a clergyman's daughter, raised in an atmosphere of religious debate, she recognized the importance of scriptural understanding. Certainly, Anne Hutchinson believed in liberties we take for granted today. She did not believe that ministers should wield unquestioned power over their listeners. "It was never in my heart to slight any man," she later said in her own defense, "But only that man should be kept in his own place and not set in the room of God."

More radical still, for Anne's time, was her conviction that God's presence could be felt directly by any believer. The clergy were not necessary to mediate the worshiper's experience of divine grace. She was truly the daughter of a defiant religious era.

For about two years, Anne Hutchinson opened her home weekly for prayer and discussion. Her husband continued to prosper; her family continued to grow. In 1636, she gave birth to her fourteenth child, a son christened Zuriel. The large and lively Hutchinson clan must have evoked a good deal of admiration—and, no doubt, a certain amount of envy. It was only a matter of time before Anne would be questioned by the ministers, few of whom commanded Anne's popularity.

First, the ministers stringently criticized Mistress Hutchinson's "unauthorized" meetings. The initial reason for their opposition was "concern for the faithful," who might be "confused" about doctrinal points.

Anne, undeterred, continued to hold her meetings. The pressure on her increased. The clergy reminded Anne of the Pauline text stating that women in Corinth should keep silent in church.

Hutchinson noted that she spoke in her own home and countered with other texts from Galatians and Titus, allowing older women to instruct the younger.

Meanwhile, Anne's own family began to divide over the issue of her meetings. Soon, they knew, further action would be taken. Will Hutchinson remained loyal and supportive of his wife. But Anne's oldest daughter, ironically named Faith, expressed anger over the increasingly tense situation. Other voices were raised at the long dining table in the house on School Street. And so Anne Hutchinson approached a crisis of conscience. The Massachusetts Synod was meeting in Cambridge. If it banned her meetings, would she comply—or defy them?

It is highly unlikely that Anne would have undertaken defiance without careful thought. She was not only the daughter of a minister—she was the daughter of a minister silenced by his own Anglican church for his opinions. Anne would have experienced the effects of defiance on her own household. She admired her father and must have watched him struggle with his decision. Then she lived through that decision's aftermath. Perhaps that was hard on her family; perhaps, however, it was harder still when her father was in a state of anguished indecision.

Anne herself was the devoted parent of many children. Clearly, her family was important to her, and she had given much of her time to nurturing her brood. If she took a stand for conscience, she knew, her family would feel the repercussions. Still, Anne had seen her father's distress when he tried to go against his conscience. Perhaps he had spoken of this with her, his eldest child, whom he had personally educated. Francis Marbury had taught his daughter how to plumb the Scriptures, how to study, and how to think. In the end, he had chosen integrity of belief and faithfulness to conscience, despite the predictable consequences.

Her father must have been on Anne Hutchinson's mind as she wrestled with her own choices. When the Synod banned her meetings, her situation was ironically similar to her father's dilemma. In the historical novel *Witnesses*, I tried to imagine Anne's struggle. I envisioned her thinking aloud with her friend, one hot summer night in her Boston home.

"Where is that line, Nell?" this imagined Anne says, "Where? Where does it become selfishness to stand on principle at all costs? Where is that place, that tiny place, where fidelity to conscience turns into arrogance? How shall I weigh this, having no experience of sainthood, no extraordinary powers to help me....?"

The only "extraordinary power" she could turn to was God. Everything we know about her life places God at its center. Her decision must have been made in the course of prayerful consideration. Her husband would not give her a command or make the decision for her. As a man of his era, Will Hutchinson gave his wife the extraordinary liberty of making her own choice in her own way.

The matter was between her and God—and we know her ultimate decision. Despite the objections of her daughter, Anne Hutchinson continued to hold her meetings, defying the order of the Massachusetts Synod. She well understood the inevitable consequences of her stand for the principles of religious liberty and freedom of speech.

In the autumn of 1637, three and a half years after her arrival in Boston, Anne was arrested and tried on the charge of "sedition." She had disobeyed her elders and, according to them, had spread "abominable" teachings throughout the community, especially among the women. These teachings, in fact, were referred to as a "contagion." Anne Hutchinson's civil trial, held in the meeting house, must have been a major event. Everyone would have crowded into the barn-like building or peered in through its windows.

Before her neighbors, friends, and enemies, then, Hutchinson was relentlessly interrogated. I imagine her, a lone female figure, standing before a row of grim-faced magistrates garbed in iron-gray. She was defendant and defender, adroitly using her wit for long debates with her accusers.

The outcome of the proceedings, however, was never really in question. One woman could not be permitted to best a bench of magistrates, no matter how sound her arguments were. In addition, she was accused of endangering the stability of the new colony by voicing and creating differences of opinion—rights so fiercely guarded by the United States Constitution a century and a half later. Finally, Anne Hutchinson turned on the biased court itself.

According to John Winthrop's transcript of the proceedings, the defendant's voice rang out: "You have no power over my body, neither can you do me any harm," she said. "I fear none but the great Jehovah, which hath foretold me of these things, and I do verily believe he will deliver me out of your hands...." Her fiery words must have caused a shocked silence and then a stir among the onlookers, who could not have expected such an outspoken stance, especially from a woman.

The magistrates' response to Anne's speech was brutal. One by one, they attacked, calling her a heretic and a tool of Satan, with "the guile of a Jesuit"—a great slur, indeed, from the Puritans. "You have stepped out of your place," snapped one minister. "You have rather been a husband than a wife, a preacher than a hearer, and a magistrate than a subject." At last, the sentence was pronounced. "You are banished out of our jurisdictions and shall be held in prison until the court shall send you away."

Throughout the winter of 1637–38, Anne Hutchinson was locked in the frigid attic of Thomas Weld, minister of Roxbury.

Will Hutchinson rode out into the wilderness, seeking new land for the family beyond the colony. At forty-six, ill and weakened by her fifteenth pregnancy, Hutchinson was given little in the way of comfort. While imprisoned, Anne did receive some visits from family and friends; she also endured many visits from members of the clergy, trying to force a recantation. Some sources state that, in her weakened state, Anne did sign some form of recantation while she waited to be set free.

In the spring of 1638, Boston Church took one further action to damage Anne Hutchinson's self-esteem and reputation. Immediately after her release from Weld's attic, Hutchinson was subjected to an ecclesiastical trial in the meeting house. This time, the assembled ministers of the colony, from Salem to Ipswich, were the judges and jury.

Among them was John Cotton, once the Hutchinsons' minister in Alford, Lincolnshire, and Anne's mentor. He, too, joined his peers in their stand against his former protégé. Did Anne truly recant and repent? she was asked. What, precisely, did she believe now? "I believe what I have always believed," Anne Hutchinson declared. "My judgment has not altered." Any recantation she may have made was now nullified.

Pastor Wilson made the final pronouncement: "I think we are bound upon this ground to remove her from us by excommunication, seeing she does prevaricate in her words." He then began the solemn pronunciation of excommunication over her: "Forasmuch as you, Mistress Hutchinson, have highly transgressed and offended and troubled the church with your errors and have drawn always many a poor soul..."

Anne stood up before the pulpit as he continued:

"I do cast you out and deliver you up to Satan and account you from this time forth to be a heathen and a publican. I command you in the name of Jesus Christ to withdraw yourself as a leper from this congregation."

Anne Hutchinson turned and regarded the whole congregation, its magistrates, and ministers. "The Lord does not judge as man judges," she spoke out. "It is better to be cast out of the church than to deny Christ." She walked up the aisle, accompanied only by her friend, Mary Dyer, and together they stepped through the open doors and out into the sunlight.

After a hazardous journey, Anne and her younger children joined Will Hutchinson in Rhode Island. Soon after the family was reunited, Anne suffered a difficult late-term miscarriage. This event was reported from the pulpit of Boston Church; the miscarriage was interpreted as a sign of divine judgment against the banished heretic and a vindication of her excommunication.

In time, Anne Hutchinson recovered from her physical trials. With her husband, she co-founded Portsmouth, Rhode Island, known for its religious tolerance. William Hutchinson was elected governor of the colony until his death in 1642. His widow, fearing the long reach of her enemies in Massachusetts, moved her family into Dutch territory, near what is now Eastchester, New York. There, in August 1643, Indians massacred the Hutchinson family.

In Boston Church, this massacre was interpreted as yet another sign of God's wrathful judgment. Centuries passed before a statue was placed before the Statehouse honoring Anne Hutchinson's conscientious stand for religious liberty in the formative years of America.

....

Questions for Reflection and Discussion

1. How would you define Anne Hutchinson's example?
2. What sustained her more than anything?
3. Was she motivated by faith, conscience—or ego?
   Could she have been motivated by all three?
4. When does personal courage put others at risk?
5. What do you think of Anne's choice: family or principle?
6. Do you think she was "driven" or "called?"
   Could she have been both?
7. What can we learn about the cost of discipleship
   from Anne Hutchinson?
8. Do we need Hutchinson's kind of commitment today?
9. Would you stand against your community for a principle?
10. Where is "the moment of truth" for this heroine?

Mary Fisher of Yorkshire
1623-1698

Mary Fisher in audience
with the sultan of Turkey, 1658,
relaying a message from God.

The silent girl approached the sultan. In seconds, he could order her death. With his nod, it would be done. Instead, the Turkish ruler beckoned to the young Englishwoman. His guards had conveyed her purpose: "She had something to declare to him from the great God." Intrigued, the sultan granted her an audience. "Bearing God's message in her heart, her life within her hand," the girl had entered the royal presence, against prudent advice.

This man was the Muslim monarch, Mahomet IV, of Turkey. She was a Quaker serving girl, Mary Fisher of Yorkshire. In her plain gray dress, she stood alone amid the splendid Eastern court. No one else had dared to accompany her. The English consul had warned her, "By all means forbear."

Mary, however, felt God's presence with her. Indeed, it was he who had prompted her to make this long journey, so that the sultan would hear the good news: God's light was with everyone and illuminated each soul.

As Mary Fisher stood before the sultan, interpreters and officials were assembled, as for an ambassador. Mary appeared to have such a role. Why else would she have traveled thousands of miles to deliver a message? One wonders if she felt any fear, any hesitation, any failure of nerve. Perhaps she reminded herself what she had endured in the past, on more familiar ground than this.

Mary Fisher was eighteen when she heard George Fox preach to Richard Tomlinson's household, where Mary was employed. Fox, the founder of the Society of Friends (known as Quakers) had spoken with such eloquence that the Tomlinsons and their servants were convinced of his beliefs: God is light, present to everyone without mediation by the clergy. Even an uneducated serving girl like Mary could experience this light.

Fox had referred to John's Gospel to substantiate his beliefs. Had Jesus not said, "I am the Light of the World?" Mary had been amazed and moved to know that God could be with one of lowly estate; one such as herself. Something fundamental changed for Mary Fisher that day.

Mary began to see herself from a different perspective. Jesus had reached out to the lowly, the "little ones," the oppressed. Of little account to society, Mary discovered herself anew as a child of God, a daughter of the King of Kings. How then could she turn away?

Her subsequent actions evidence her change in self-perception and her costly decision to put herself at risk for what she now believed. This quiet servant took a dangerous stand—but throughout her new life, she seems to have felt empowered by her choice. Once a "nobody," she felt increasingly strengthened; enabled to face suffering—and a sultan—unfazed.

Out in the streets of York, she preached to all who would listen—and was arrested on the charge of "speaking to a priest." For this, she was convicted and sent to prison with other Quakers, who gave her further instruction about their teachings.

In 1653, after she was set at liberty again, Mary immediately went back to preaching in public. With a friend, she first traveled through East Anglia where Elizabeth Hooten, the first Quaker minister, had been jailed. Mary must have noted the Quakers' courage of their convictions and their examples may have heartened her. With a friend, Mary Fisher undertook a new mission: to preach the Gospel at the renowned Sussex College.

William Pickery, the mayor, received a complaint from the college that two women, uninvited, were speaking there. They were arrested and questioned. When they were asked for their names, their response was perceived as disrespectful. Their names, they said, quoting Scripture, were written "in the book of life" as laborers of the Gospel (Philippians 4:3). Pickery's pride was ruffled. Angered, he demanded to know who the women's husbands were. Mary and her friend replied, "We have no husbands but Jesus Christ."

Now furious, Pickery swore out a warrant for the public flogging of these "preachers." With an extra twist of malice, the mayor ordered that the women be taken to the market cross in the town's center, where they were to be whipped until they bled. As they stood before the cross, Mary and her friend were stripped to their waists. Half naked, they were attached to a post. The constable obeyed his orders to the letter. The women were flogged until their bodies ran with blood.

Mary showed no fear before or during her ordeal. As the lash came down across their backs, the women kept each other's courage up by singing hymns and praising God who strengthened them. When the whippings concluded, the women knelt and prayed forgiveness for their tormenter.

Their example, in turn, inspired others when this incident was reported by Joseph Besse in *A Collection of the Sufferings of the People Called Quakers for the Testimony of Good Conscience*. No one came forward to help the bleeding women and they were summarily run out of town. The entire incident was reported in a widely circulated pamphlet, *The First Persecution*.

Undeterred by this experience and another, later imprisonment, Mary Fisher continued to model her ministry on the example of the early Christians. The Apostle Paul, she knew, had been beaten and jailed many times for the sake of the Gospel. Perpetua and Blandina and many other Christian women had been martyred. In Mary's times, if others had lukewarm faith, hers need not be the same.

"Mary is much grown in power since her last imprisonment," wrote a fellow Quaker, Thomas Aldam, who had been jailed with her. In 1655, at the age of thirty-two, Mary sailed for America with an older woman who served as her companion. When their ship stopped in Barbados, Mary wrote to George Fox: "My dear Father—let me not be forgotten of thee but let thy praise be for me that I may continue faithful to the end. If any of our Friends be free to come over they may be serviceable here as many are convinced and many desire to know the way. I rest, thy child begotten into the truth."

Mary would need all the prayers that George Fox could offer. From Barbados, the ship, *the Swallow*, carried her to Boston, which had just passed legislation that strictly outlawed Quakers from the

Massachusetts Bay Colony. The Boston elders were convinced that Quaker doctrine was an evil contagion that must not be allowed to enter Puritan jurisdictions.

Consequently, Mary and her companion, Ann Austin, were not permitted to disembark in Boston. Their trunks were ransacked, their books were torched, their Bibles snatched away. Finally the women were permitted to leave the ship, only to be thrown into prison. There they were stripped and searched carefully for "witches' marks." Not a mark was found. Even so, to keep the Quaker "contagion" at bay, and to prevent the women from speaking to anyone, their prison window was blocked with boards. There was no light, no air—and no food. The Boston magistrates seem to have settled

Quaker tapestry of Mary Fisher

on a starvation policy for the prisoners while they decided what to do with them. The courage of one Bostonian, Nicholas Upsall, saved the women's lives. Bribing their jailor, Upsall smuggled food in to Mary and Ann until they were finally deported, first to Barbados and then to England.

One wonders how Mary Fisher endured the rigors of floggings, humiliations, imprisonments, and two ocean crossings. This would have been enough to make most people quit, no matter how faithful they were.

Mary Fisher, however, remained true to her conscience. Her greatest mission lay ahead of her, prompted by her conscience and defying all convention. Again, Mary's courage and her trials seem to mirror the Apostle Paul's. Her apparent calm and cheer may indicate strong inner spiritual communion and support. There is no indication of mental instability in Mary's case. It is difficult for us to understand the early Quakers' zeal without seeing it within the context of the times.

In the wake of the Reformation, there was continuing religious turmoil and a reaction against clerical abuses. While Quakers were preaching in English towns, Presbyterians were preaching in Scottish fields—and both denominations suffered. It was a time when religious causes were so passionate, their adherents acted with the fervor of the early church.

Again led by her conscience, Mary felt called to another faraway land. This time, it was Islamic Turkey, thousands of miles away. With five other Quakers, she sailed for Greece. From there she went on alone. When she arrived in Smyrna, however, the British consul discouraged Mary from continuing and booked passage for her on a ship bound for Venice.

She disembarked as soon as the ship came into its next port and from there she set out on her own to cross Greece and Macedonia—

about six hundred miles. Her destination was Constantinople. She records no fear of traveling in foreign territories as a woman alone.

We receive a pastoral impression of Mary as she walked along the Greek coastline, perhaps dazzled by the intense blue of the sea and the brilliance of the sun, until she came to the mountains of Thrace. With some assistance from local peoples, she crossed this barrier. One source reports that she was assisted by Bedouins and shepherds who shared water and simple shelter with her. Somehow, she managed to make a little progress each day.

She could speak no Arabic or Aramaic, she wore foreign dress, and most curious of all, for a lone traveler, was her gender. Wherever she went, she told her hosts that she was carrying "a message to the king from the Most High God." A commentator suggests that her "credentials" were accepted, or her "mission" was that of a harmless, itinerant lunatic. Was she? Perhaps her odyssey seems so to us. To Mary, it may have been high adventure, far beyond the dreams of a below-stairs servant girl in Yorkshire.

It is also possible that Mary Fisher was on a genuine religious pilgrimage, one of biblical proportions. As she walked, she may have reflected on the faithfulness of Abraham and Sarah, who followed God's call to a new land. Perhaps she meditated on the Christian apostles' tireless travels. Mary Fisher had ample time to reflect on the oneness of all who followed God's call for the sake of the Gospel.

It is noteworthy that Mary Fisher was following in the steps of Francis of Assisi, who also felt called to visit a Turkish sultan— against all prudent advice. To us, such a pilgrimage seems pictur-esque, perhaps naive. It has the ring of Don Quixote's excursions. To Francis and to Mary, however, such journeys were spiritually im-pelled, as were those of Moses and Miriam, Jacob and Rebecca, and Jesus of Nazareth, who journeyed toward Jerusalem and the cross.

With him came faithful women, mentioned in the Gospel of Luke, and perhaps Mary felt herself close to those earliest of followers.

Whatever went through Mary's mind, she managed to reach the sultan of Turkey, who had relocated his court from Constantinople to Adrianople, a fact she must have gleaned from the local population. Mary was clear about her mission. She had come thousands of miles to deliver a message from God. She was a woman. She was alone. These factors were so extraordinary, perhaps they elicited curiosity. Mary's appearance certainly was a novelty. And perhaps there was something miraculous about this visit.

Mahomet IV was housed in a lavish tent high on a hilltop, looking down over an encampment of twenty thousand soldiers. Spreading out before Mary, this must have presented an overwhelming sight. Even so, Mary was able to contact a high official, the grand vizier, to arrange for an audience with the great monarch. She waited in the city while the decision was made.

How had she passed on her own, over such a great distance? Maybe God was with this calm, fearless woman after all. The grand vizier sent a dispatch to Mary Fisher. The interview was granted for the next day. No doubt, she prepared for it with prayer and meditation. She consulted no one and approached the sultan's encampment alone.

With customary honor due the sultan, Mary was ushered into Mahomet's presence. The golds and crimsons of his hanging silks must have leapt out at her. His officials flanked him as they did when the sultan received an ambassador.

Three interpreters stepped forward, and one asked Mary if what he heard was true: Did she have a message from the Lord God? Mary asserted that she did. There was a silence, it is reported, while Mary waited for the sultan to respond. The interpreters murmured. "Speak on," was Mahomet's reply. He urged her not to be afraid.

With great gravity, the whole assembly gave heed to her earnest ministry. There is no record of what she said, but she would have spoken of God's light: how it illumines everyone and how God's presence can be known directly by everyone. She may have quoted John, the favored Gospel among Quakers.

When she finished her speech, there was another silence. Would the sultan's guards draw their swords? No one moved. Through the interpreters, the sultan asked Mary if she had anything more to say. She asked if he had understood her. Again through the interpreters, the monarch replied, "Yea, every word, and it is truth!" Mary was invited to stay in the sultan's realm but she demurred.

She had delivered her message; now she must return to her country. An escort was offered. This, too, Mary declined with gratitude, "trusting in the Lord alone." The sultan said "they could not but respect such a one, as should take so much pains to come to them so far as from England."

Then he asked what she thought of his prophet, Mohammed. Mary said "she knew him not, but Christ, the Son of God, who was the Light of the World, and enlightened every man coming into the world, him she knew." There was an amicable silence.

With cordiality she departed and began her long journey home. The image of this British woman, dressed in plain gray, and the Ottoman sultan, arrayed in silks, is a powerful one, especially for our contemporary world. A little-known event, it is nonetheless an historic one amid the conflicts of "the crescent and the cross." This meeting transcends the delineations of race, religion, and gender. It was made possible by the gracious sultan, to be sure, but also by the conscience and courage of a servant—a word that carries an ironically double connotation in this case.

No one's belief system was swayed that day in 1658, but in the end, something more important and iconic occurred. A sense of that is imparted in Mary Fisher's letter to another Quaker when she returned home: "I bore my testimony for the Lord before the king unto whom I was sent, and he was very noble unto me...and he and all that were about him received words of truth without contradiction....They do dread the name of God, many of them, and I as his messenger....There is a love begotten in me towards them which is endless." If that love was endless, then Mary Fisher must have carried that love with her for the rest of her long life. Now in her middle years, she finally married another Quaker, also a preacher, as well as a mariner.

William Bayly was lost at sea, but Mary remarried and moved with her new husband, John Crosse, to Charleston, South Carolina. She became the mother of three children and worked for Quaker causes until the end of her life. Mary Fisher is buried in the Quaker Burial Ground in Charleston and is honored as one of "The Valiant Sixty," the first missionaries of the Society of Friends.

Questions for Reflection and Discussion

1. How would you define Mary Fisher's example?
2. What sustained her more than anything?
3. Do you see her as motivated by faith? Was she a fanatic?
4. Do you think she was an adventurer or a faith-based preacher?
5. Was Mary Fisher's "mission" egocentric or heroic?
6. Do you think she was "driven" or "called?" Could she have been both?
7. Do you think Mary Fisher was right to follow a "higher law?"
8. Where do we need Fisher's kind of commitment today?
9. Would you have expressed your religious beliefs if you knew you would be flogged?
10. Where is "the moment of truth" for this heroine?

Harriet Tubman of Maryland
1820?-1913

Born a slave in Maryland, Harriet Ross Tubman had a recurring dream: "I was flying over cotton fields and cornfields and the corn was ripe, its tassels waving golden-brown in the sun," she recalled. "I came to a river and I flew over that. I came to a mountain and I flew over that. But I always came to a barrier I couldn't fly over...." Then, just as she was sinking down, angelic figures on the other side reached out their hands to her and pulled her across.

This dream pervaded Harriet's childhood. Along with other visionary experiences, it informed her girlhood. Even so, many years would pass before she could escape from slavery. Once she was free, she sensed God calling her to a larger vocation. Risking all, Tubman returned South and soon began her new mission: Now she must reach out to others and pull them across that "barrier." She obeyed her summons—again and again. Within one decade she personally rescued some three hundred souls from bondage.

To the slave owners, Tubman was an outlaw with a reward posted for her capture—dead or alive. To the slaves, Tubman was a savior with a reward waiting in heaven. Harriet herself was disinterested in this debate. She quietly followed her conscience, breaking the law of the land for the sake of a higher law. This, she believed was God's own law, nothing less. Didn't the Scriptures bear her out? "Tell Pharaoh to let my people go," the Lord had commanded Moses. "I come to proclaim liberty to the captives," Jesus had announced. "When you do it to the least of these...you do it to me," God seemed to be telling Harriet Ross Tubman.

It was not always so clear to her. As the property of Edward Brodess, a tobacco grower near Cambridge, Maryland, she watched her sister taken away on a chain gang. After that traumatic sight, Harriet became a willful and "uppity" child. Small, stocky, and strong, she was devout—and defiant. For a long time, she thought only of her own freedom and planned to run away. Her first attempt got her as far as the plantation's pigpen, where she hid out for a day.

At sixteen, Harriet's situation took a more serious turn. She decided to help a friend escape the plantation, but paid a costly price for her complicity. To distract the overseer, Harriet confronted him. Infuriated, he hurled a heavy iron weight at her and struck her in the head.

Unconscious and bleeding, Harriet lay close to death for weeks. Gradually, she recovered her strength, but her injury left her with a lifelong form of epilepsy. This lowered her value as "property," however, and ensured that she would not be sold away from her family.

Harriet did not give up on God—or on her freedom. She asked to be "hired out" to other planters, working extra hours for small sums of money. If she could not run off, she reasoned, she would save her coins and purchase her freedom one day. Throughout the 1840s, she labored as long as there was daylight and sold her garden produce at the Cambridge market.

Adversity only strengthened her resolve. In a mule's harness, Harriet pulled a heavy barge several yards at her master's command—for his guests' entertainment. After this humiliation, Harriet presented her savings to her owner, demanding her freedom in return. Her master only laughed and raised Harriet's price.

Temporarily discouraged, Harriet Ross married John Tubman, a free black man who gave his wife a tantalizing taste of liberty. For a time, the union was happy but eventually it deteriorated. It is hard to know what made the marriage break down. Harriet spent most of her time working to build up her "freedom money," and John traveled often, doing odd jobs around the county. Perhaps John accused Harriet of neglect; perhaps she accused him of infidelity. Whatever the marital dynamics were, Harriet left her husband and her family one night in 1849. "I reasoned it out this way," she later told her biographer. "I had only had rights to two things: to go free or to die. I would have one or the other." Defying the law, she made good on her decision.

Harriet Ross Tubman "lit out" alone—or so it seemed. She felt God's presence with her and the presence of her earthly father as well. Ben Ross was wise in the ways of nature, and he had passed his knowledge on to his daughter. Harriet knew how to follow the

North Star and the moss growing on the north side of the trees. She waded against the current of the Choptank River to kill her scent, especially when a search party's dogs pursued her. It was during this high-risk flight that Harriet Tubman discovered the fabled Underground Railroad.

Despite the legends, no train or tracks ran beneath the earth as a kind of nineteenth-century subway. Instead, there was a greater marvel: A network of committed, conscience-driven people of faith, working together for the cause of human freedom. They hid slaves in designated "safe houses" and secretly transported fugitives in wagons rolling North. Foodstuffs and faked passes, disguises, and tickets were passed along in market baskets and boxes.

Most active on this "Railroad" were Quakers and free African Americans; they provided passes, food, and tickets on actual trains for disguised runaways. With the code name "Moses," Harriet Tubman would become a major figure on the Eastern branch of the Underground Railroad. Early on, however, when she was running for her life, Harriet could not have imagined her future calling.

On this, her first journey, the famed Quaker abolitionist, Thomas Garrett, sheltered Harriet in Wilmington, Delaware, and drove her toward the Pennsylvania border. From Garrett's carriage, Tubman proceeded on foot, walking into the dawn. When she reached the stone marker on the state line, she took a breath—and stepped across.

For some moments, then, she stood very still. "I looked at my hands," she recalled, "to see if I was the same person now I was free.

"The sun came like gold through the trees and there was such a glory over everything...." In Philadelphia, Tubman immersed herself in the work of the Anti-Slavery Society, guided by the renowned African American abolitionist, William Still. With Still, Harriet ministered to newly arrived runaway slaves, most of them ragged, starving, ill, and destitute. The sight of them stirred her spirit and spurred her on to work closely with these refugees.

She remembered watching an old man die, smiling, in a church pew, simply grateful that he had lived to be free. Again, Harriet was profoundly moved. In the recesses of her soul, her calling was beginning to take form.

In 1850, Harriet Tubman made plans to go South again, despite the danger and William Still's warnings. Undeterred, she set out to rescue her parents and her brothers. Her immediate family was Harriet Tubman's only concern when she left on that first perilous journey below the Mason-Dixon line. With high anticipation, she traveled mostly by night, reversing her earlier escape route.

But when Harriet reached the old Brodess plantation, she found her family absent. Her parents and brothers had been "hired out" to other planters all over the county and no one knew exactly where they were—or when they might return. At that point, her dangerous journey seemed to be in vain.

Stunned and deeply disappointed, Harriet must have turned to God in prayer. And sometime during that first night, alone and lost, Harriet Tubman had a life-changing conversion experience. Her God-given calling came clear to her at last. She had come through great danger to rescue one set of "kinfolk," but she had not grasped the fullness of her mission until her hour of despair. This disappointment was a sign: *all* those in bondage were her people. *All* those in bondage were her family.

Harriet knew then that she could not simply turn around and safeguard her own freedom. Nor could she limit her rescues to her parents and brothers. Her mission was to help anyone who desired freedom for as long as God called her to serve him. The mission was accepted; Harriet Tubman put her life in God's hands, defied all danger, and followed her conscience—that night and many nights thereafter.

A decade of dangerous, dedicated service began for Harriet Tubman. Repeatedly, she slipped into Maryland to rescue more of her people. She crept through the slave quarters, whispering at windows, singing snatches of songs, crouching by cabin fires. Everyone knew her, trusted her, and listened to her stories about that great unknown: "The North."

After making her rounds, she awaited anyone who might "want to travel." And there, in the dark, Tubman formed her first escape party. In a line, nine fugitives moved in silence, following the woman they called "Moses." With the help of her contacts on the Underground Railroad, that jubilant group of fugitive slaves eluded their pursuers and safely crossed the line into Pennsylvania—and freedom.

Her conscience would let her do no less.

Tubman designed and conducted about twenty rescue "missions" to Maryland, the territory she knew best. All twenty missions succeeded, despite adverse weather, intense pursuit, and the rising fee advertised for Harriet's capture. "I never ran my train off the track," Tubman later said. "And I never lost a passenger." She believed that God guided her on every journey. "I talk with the Lord every day, the way you talk with a friend," she told her biographer. Tubman's sense of divine communion was central to her life. When scouting a plantation, her signal songs to the slaves were "Steal Away to Jesus" and "Go Down Moses."

Harriet was as practical as she was mystical. Her journeys were plotted in detail and her "passengers" were treated firmly. No one could turn back once an escape was in progress. Tubman carried a pistol and used it to shove recalcitrant runaways when the need arose. "Dead folk tell no tales," she would remind her followers. "Keep moving." And move they did, often on Christmas; while the planters were celebrating, Tubman would get a day's jump on the inevitable pursuers.

After the Fugitive Slave Act was passed in 1850, runaways could be captured anywhere in the United States. Tubman was not deterred; she escorted her parties to the Canadian border. Eventually, Harriet did rescue her aging parents, settling them in the town of Saint Catherine's, Canada, then in Auburn, New York. Her father and mother may have assumed their daughter would finally settle down with them in their new home. Perhaps her freed brothers assumed this was their sister's role. We cannot know the family dynamics, but we do know the expectations of the era. Harriet stayed with her parents for an interval, but her conscience was challenged.

Harriet could not rest while so many of her people waited to be saved. Soon she was on her way down to Maryland's eastern shore once again. From the pattern of Tubman's life, I sense that she returned to action because she felt called to do so. There are no indications that she neglected her parents, whom she supported for the remainder of their lives. Nor are there any signs that she regarded her work as high adventure, selfishly embraced. For the woman called Moses, her work was her God-given mission.

We can derive some insight on this point from the great African American orator, Frederick Douglass, himself a former slave. On August 26, 1868, Douglass wrote the following letter to his friend, Harriet Tubman: "The difference between us is very marked. Most that I have done and suffered in the service of our cause has been in public, and I have received much encouragement at every step of the way. You, on the other hand, have labored in a private way. I have wrought in the day—you in the night.

"I have had the applause of the crowd and the satisfaction that comes of being approved by the multitude, while the most that you have done has been witnessed by a few trembling, scarred, and foot-sore bondmen and women, whom you have led out of the house of bondage, and whose heartfelt 'God bless you' has been your only reward. The midnight sky and the silent stars have been the witness of your devotion to freedom...."

Although Harriet Tubman was a dynamic speaker at abolition-ists' meetings, her main focus remained on each small "exodus" she generated. One wonders if she ever grew frustrated with her method. When activist and militant John Brown consulted her, she was receptive to his vision of radical change. At that time, Brown sought to incite a mass "exodus" of runaway slaves to the mountains of Virginia. He was not then an advocate of violent rebellion.

After Brown's failed raid on Harpers Ferry in West Virginia, Harriet did not try to replicate his original plan. Grieving for Brown, she returned to the Underground Railroad. Tubman would have agreed with Mother Teresa of Calcutta, whom Harriet predated by more than two hundred years: "We must do small things with great love." This is precisely what Harriet Tubman did until the outbreak of the Civil War.

The work of the Underground Railroad ceased as battle lines formed. Once again, Harriet could not remain nested in her Auburn home. Throughout the war, she served as an unofficial spy, based in Hilton Head, South Carolina, and participated in a least one raid on the Combahee River.

It is certain that she stayed awake on "Watch Night," December 31, 1862, as African Americans waited for the Emancipation Proc-lamation to go into effect at twelve. Tubman continued to work for the military as nurse, cook, or spy until General Robert E. Lee surrendered in 1865.

Because of her gender, Tubman received no remuneration or pension for her service, even after influential friends petitioned

Congress on her behalf. Nearly destitute after the Civil War's end, Tubman supported her household by selling garden produce at market. This was not enough, however, when she could not make the payments on her house.

Sarah Bradford, an Auburn educator, wrote out Tubman's dictated autobiography and friends put the book into print. Its sales generated enough income to safeguard Harriet's home. Its door was always open to anyone who needed a place to stay, and its garden produce continued to be sold. The brilliant Underground Railroad "conductor" was generous, often beyond her means.

Harriet spent the rest of her long life in relative obscurity. She remained an active member of her church community and continued in her life of prayer. In 1868, she married Nelson Davis, a war veteran who died of tuberculosis. It is ironic that his widow finally received a military pension at his death, although it was not her own.

In 1878, Harriet was able to found the John Brown Home for ill and indigent African Americans. There she died peacefully, surrounded by hymn-singing friends, on the evening of March 10, 1913. Harriet Tubman was buried with military honors in Auburn's Fort Hill Cemetery. Today, schools and libraries bear her name and pass along her story.

Questions for Reflection and Discussion

1. How would you define Harriet Tubman's example?
2. What sustained her more than anything?
3. Was she motivated by faith—or anger?
   Could she have been motivated by both?
4. Did her courage put others at risk?
5. Was Harriet Tubman's "mission" egocentric or heroic?
6. Do you think she was "driven" or "called?"
   Could she have been both?
7. Do you think Tubman was right to follow a "higher law?"
8. Do we need Tubman's kind of commitment today?
9. Would you have hidden a runaway slave or worked
   on the Underground Railroad?
10. Where is "the moment of truth" for this heroine?

Mary "Mother" Jones
of Chicago
1837?-1930

"My address is like my shoes. It travels with me," said the small, silvery-voiced woman in the black dress. For much of her life, Mary Harris Jones had no fixed address.

After losing all, she lived "wherever there is a fight against wrong." Her home was in train cars, depots, boarding houses, and occasionally in jails across the United States. With her sweet-faced demeanor, her graying hair, her spectacles, and her black garb, she resembled an aging auntie, not a labor advocate.

"Mother Jones," as she came to be known, was called "The Miners' Angel"—and "the most dangerous woman in America." That last epithet always pleased and amused her.

Raised as a Catholic, she was often critical of religious hypocrisy and, often, the clergy. Her ministry would lie outside traditional Christian church organizations, although her speeches often referred to God and the Scriptures. The teachings of Jesus and the prophets permeated her most powerful talks; she saw herself aligned with the biblical concern for the oppressed. When called to help miners in West Virginia, she exclaimed: "When I cross to the other side, I shall tell God Almighty about West Virginia."

Who was she, this five-foot spitfire? Where had she come from, before she appeared in the coalfields of America? She was Mary Harris Jones, born to working-class patriots in Cork City, Ireland. Her rebel ancestors were part of her personal history—as was tragedy.

As a girl, she survived the devastation caused by the Great Famine and watched the starving Irish peasants eat grass. Nearly three million Irish people were lost to death or emigration; the Harris family was fortunate to reach Canada. Soon they moved to Michigan and became United States citizens. Mary was always extremely proud of this and considered it a great honor.

Mary trained as a teacher at Saint Mary's Academy in Monroe. In the classroom, she found the nuns' rules too strict. To her parents' horror, she quit her parish post and struck out on her own for Chicago and Memphis. This defiant behavior was improper for a nice girl of Mary's era and caused an irreparable rift in her family.

In Memphis, Mary Harris met and married George Jones, a trained iron molder and a proud member of the nascent union, The Knights of Labor. Like many workers less skilled than he, George was on the job six days a week, for ten hours a day. Working conditions were extremely dangerous. Wages were low; benefits were nil. The company owners ruled the workers as barons ruled serfs, without any restraints, answering to nobody. Even so, George was a trained craftsman. He and his fellow workers deserved better conditions and higher pay.

Mary must have absorbed George's passion for the working class, as the couple settled into a crowded Memphis neighborhood, called "Pinch." She read the Knights of Labor journal that arrived monthly on her doorstep. Their marriage was a happy one, and the household kept growing. In the span of six years, the Joneses had three small children and a new baby.

Together, George and Mary, both pro-Union, survived the Civil War in Memphis. The city was captured by Union forces in 1863. Together, they also mourned the death of President Abraham Lincoln.

Meanwhile, the Jones's domestic world remained stable. And then, in one week, Mary's family was gone. A Yellow Fever epidemic struck the "Pinch" neighborhood in Memphis in the late 1860s and in quick succession, the four Jones children died, followed by their father. Mary remembers sitting alone through nights of grief; no neighbor could come to her. She remained estranged from parents and siblings. She must have felt utterly alone.

In the end, it was George's "brothers" from the Knights of Labor who came to her, with their wives, and saw that George received a proper burial. They even draped their union charter in black crepe for a month. The Knights' motto was, "An injury to one is an injury to all." Mary never forgot.

It is hard to imagine how Mary Jones survived this staggering tragedy. She certainly could not stay in Memphis and, in time, relocated to Chicago, where she had lived before. Through what must have been a great act of will, Mary called on her earliest training, sewing, to set herself up in business as a seamstress and dressmaker with her own shop.

Sewing gowns for wealthy women on Lake Shore Drive, Mary watched the ragged poor through the mansions' windows. Perhaps she thought back to the Knights of Labor motto.

Her conscience began to stir—but before she could think anything through, her life was thrown into crisis for a third time. In the summer of 1871, the Great Chicago Fire totally destroyed Mary's new home and shop. Her fabrics went up in flames. Her sewing machine melted. Everything, once more, was gone. She must have wandered, dazed, through the devastated city.

Now she was a destitute, widowed, childless, homeless woman. By night, she slept in a church with other dispossessed people. By day, she stood in its soup line. Now, firsthand, she understood how the dispossessed felt. And now, she faced the greatest challenge of her life: despair. Mary Harris Jones had reached the watershed moment of her life. She could have taken that life. She could have gone mad or turned to the bottle. Instead, she turned her life into one of service.

Perhaps Mary was missing her husband when she sought out a new, unofficial chapter of the Knights of Labor. Every evening she went to its meetings and listened to its speakers and its members. Then she returned to her "bed" in one of the church pews. Perhaps she wondered why she had survived famine and pestilence, and fire. For what purpose? The answers came gradually. Now she was forced to think about her life—or lose it.

By the time Mary Jones had found new sewing clients, she had a room in a boarding house—and a new resolve. Surely, God had spared her life for some purpose. Now, with no responsibilities to anyone, she was free to act on that stirring of conscience she had experienced on Lake Shore Drive.

She would never marry again. She would always dress in black. And she would never establish another home. Instead, she would dedicate herself to the rights of the oppressed, especially the working poor. From them she had come, to them she had returned. She could no longer accept their plight; her lot lay with the people of the mines, the mills, the forges and the factories.

Perhaps Mary Jones reached her "point of no return" while she lived as a homeless, penniless, childless widow, sleeping on a church pew after the Great Chicago Fire. Again, history does not record her moment of decision, nor does she. But Jones was indeed at a crossroads—and she stood there alone. Still young, still pretty, she might have remarried; she might have revived her business as a seamstress. Resumption of her teaching career was another possibility.

Instead Mary Harris Jones made a radical departure from known pathways and quite literally reinvented her life. This new life would be lived for others—and she would pursue it with the solitary commitment of a celibate religious vocation.

"I belong to a class which has been robbed, exploited, and plundered down through many long centuries," she later explained. "And because I belong to that class, I have an impulse to go and help break the chains." Perhaps she drew strength from her Irish ancestors' defiance of oppression.

Mary Jones saw her defiance as a divine mandate. "The labor movement, my friends, was a command of God Almighty," she said later when she was honored at Carnegie Hall. "He commanded the prophet to redeem the Israelites who were in bondage; he organized the men into a union that led them out of the land of bondage...into the land of freedom." This, then, was the calling of Mary Harris

Jones. "An injury to one is an injury to all," she said, recalling the Knights of Labor's motto.

As she gradually learned to live with her losses, she resolved never to speak of them. For some time, she found it difficult to be around children. She felt at home at the Knights of Labor meetings; there, in the background, she watched and listened and learned about the labor movement, which was just beginning in America.

In the 1870s and 1880s, Chicago was a radical city that challenged established management practices, from the existence of sweatshops to the exploitation of railroad workers. The first major strikes in the country originated here, where Mary Jones was an apprentice to daring labor organizers, many of them Irish immigrants like her. In the labor movement she found many kindred spirits and determined rebels against injustice.

In the early 1890s, at an age when many people think of retirement, she emerged as an organizer in her own right. These were dangerous times when company owners hired armed guards to put down workers' rebellions. Mary drew on her ancestral roots for strength; she acted on her conscience well into her eighties.

In her tall hip boots and long black skirts, she tramped the coal fields from Pennsylvania to Colorado, organizing for the new United Mine Workers Union. Mary may have recalled the wretched lives of miners in County Cork. In America, to her astonishment, the situation was no better. She, as with others, had been told the streets here were paved with gold. Not for the miners. Not for the laborers, who paved the roads themselves.

Men in mining communities were housed in shacks and paid low wages by the all-powerful companies that hired them. The company "owned" them, paying workers in "scrip" that was only good at the company store. The work was dangerous and deadly, but there seemed no way out of its circularity. Mary Harris Jones began appearing at the nation's mines to provide one. She would just walk up to the mouth of a mine and strike up a conversation. Sometimes she would have a beer with "the boys." Defying the usual standards for women's behavior, she found that her approach worked.

In Arnot, Pennsylvania, she organized the miners' wives into an effective force, augmenting the strikers' efforts at the infamous Dripmouth Mine. In West Virginia, she calmly confronted armed guards, even when they threatened striking miners. The guards did not know what to make of this small, white-haired woman who clamped her hand over their rifles.

Later, Mary's efforts for miners landed her in jail more than once. When the governor of Colorado ordered her to leave the state, she defied him—and spent three months in prison, without the benefit of charges or a trial. By then, she was known nationwide as "Mother Jones." She lived with the communities she organized, enduring their living conditions firsthand.

Her seemingly tireless efforts extended to miners of all nationalities, and interpreters translated her speeches. Jones had also become a powerful force on the speaker's platform, with her fiery mix of religious and rebellious rhetoric. Small wonder that a trial lawyer exclaimed: "She is the most dangerous woman in America. She crooks her little finger and hundreds of contented men lay down their jobs."

As Mother Jones well knew, the striking workers were anything but contented. Nor was *she* contented to restrict her mission to the cause of "her boys," the miners.

Crisscrossing America, Jones slipped into other exploited communities. In the South, she slipped into mill-workers' shacks and factories, quietly "talking union" to textile workers, many of them women and children. Horrified by their twelve-hour workdays and dangerous conditions, she organized, sympathized, and made new plans. Now she wanted to focus the nation's attention on the issue of child labor. One wonders how many memories this cause evoked for Mary Jones—and how much determination those memories may have provided her.

In 1903, she designed and led a special march called a "Children's Crusade." Followed by some three hundred young millhands, Mother Jones tramped from Philadelphia to meet with President Theodore Roosevelt at his estate in Oyster Bay, New York. Most of the marchers eventually fell away, and the president refused to see Jones, who persevered to the end. The march garnered intense news coverage and spotlighted the plight of children in the workplace.

"I'm against violence," Mother Jones said. "I prefer drama." The drama of this effort made an impression on the national conscience—and eventually made a powerful contribution to later labor laws protecting children. Jones was adept at drawing public attention to unjust causes. Shortly after her death, the United States passed legislation against child labor that would have greatly pleased her.

Even as other labor organizers burnt out or gave up, Mary Jones continued her mission well into the 1920s. In Colorado, she confronted the powerful mining interests of the Rockefeller family. She also fed, clothed and comforted miners after the infamous "Ludlow Massacre," where paid thugs fired on a strike camp. In West Virginia, she persuaded local farmers to send food to starving strikers. In Wyoming, she organized copper miners, and in Milwaukee she created a union for young, immigrant women who worked as bottle-washers.

These women were young, inexperienced, and exploited. No one would take up their cause—except Mother Jones. After assessing their poor working conditions and low pay, Jones used unique tactics on the young women's behalf. At a UMW convention, she persuaded hundreds of men to boycott bottled Milwaukee beer until the women's bosses agreed to higher wages and unionization. The bosses' consent was swift.

Mother Jones said herself that she lost as many battles as she won. Nonetheless, she was beloved, feared, and frankly radical. Her dedication to her cause led to brief affiliations with Communism and the International Workers of the World, both of which she soon abandoned. Jones never abandoned her mission, however, and was seen as the mother of the American labor movement.

To the end, Mother Jones believed that people must unite in order to help one another. For her, the wide spectrum of workers comprised one extended family. As a movement's matriarch, she never wavered in her commitment to those Jesus called "the little ones" and "the least." Although she was often critical of organized religion, she always believed in the scriptural mandate to lift oppression, and she always honored God.

Some historians speculate that Jones had replaced her lost family with a larger one. One biographer suggests anger as her motivation for action. These views, however, can be seen as reductionist and rather patronizing. Mary Harris Jones overcame devastating personal adversity, reached back to her roots, and followed her conscience. Inspired by her husband's example, she defied adversity and created a mission of her own.

It is important to note that Jones labored at a time when prejudice was rampant against Irish immigrants. As an advocate for workers, Mother Jones would have seen the common addendum to job advertisements: "No Irish Need Apply." Mary Harris Jones did not allow prejudice to stop her, embitter her, or skew her focus. Her vision extended to all ethnic groups across the country she proudly adopted as her own. In fact, translators were often called in when she made speeches to people of diverse nationalities.

In her nineties, as her health failed, Mother Jones settled down with friends in Adelphi, Maryland. She continued to write and grant interviews, one of which was captured on film. In the fall of 1930, she requested the Last Rites of the Catholic Church, which she received before her death in December of that year. Some fifty thousand mourners attended her wake and lined the route of her funeral procession.

In fulfillment of her wishes, she was buried in the only union-owned and operated cemetery in the country. Created for martyred miners in Illinois, the cemetery allowed Mother Jones to be interred with "her boys." Her famous rallying call did not become her epitaph, but it is remembered: "Pray for the dead and fight like hell for the living."

Questions for Reflection and Discussion

1. How would you characterize Mother Jones's example?
2. What sustained her more than anything?
3. Was she motivated by conviction—or anger? Could she have been motivated by both?
4. How do you think she managed to defy such great adversity?
5. Was Mother Jones's "mission" egocentric or heroic?
6. Do you think she was "driven" or "called?" Could she have been both?
7. Do you see Gospel values in her life?
8. What do you think kept her going for so many years?
9. Would you have given your life for a cause or sought a more normal existence?
10. Where is "the moment of truth" for this heroine?

Corrie (1892-1983)
& Betsie (1886-1944)
ten Boom of Haarlem, Holland

Corrie ten Boom

The rap at the door came after dark. The family within must have exchanged glances. After all, it was almost time for curfew and, since the Nazi occupation, no one in Holland knew what to expect. The ten Boom family was sustained by strong Christian faith. Now its grown daughter, Cornelia, rose from her chair to answer the unusually late summons. "Come to me," Jesus had said, "all ye who are weary and heavy laden."

Corrie opened the door. Outside stood a woman with a valise. She was Jewish, she whispered. Her husband had been arrested; their son was already in hiding. The woman was afraid to return home. The ten Booms quickly drew her inside and bolted the door. Within forty-eight hours, others had slipped through the darkness to the big house at Barteljorisstraat 19. The family turned no one away, and word spread quickly through the Jewish community of Haarlem: There was a safe haven in the watchmaker's home. This home belonged to Caspar, the patriarch, sometimes called, "Haarlem's Grand Old Man."

His middle-aged daughter, called Corrie, was also a skilled watchmaker. Formally trained between 1920 and 1922, she was the first woman in Holland to receive her guild's license. Clever with her hands, she could repair all manner of clocks and watches. Through her business and her church work, she was known to many of Haarlem's people.

With his grown children, Corrie and Betsie, Caspar had lived above the family's shop throughout his life. The family had some extra bedrooms for certain "special guests." One chamber had been Nollie's, a married daughter. Despite the ten Booms' discretion, their pastor was deeply concerned. When Caspar asked him to take in a Jewish child, the pastor refused. They could all lose their lives over this, he warned. Ten Boom ignored the warning and kept the child. He was proud to have this baby as a part of his family, he said. His pastor departed, perhaps in some haste.

By day, the watch shop was open for business. By noon, Betsie had served two meals, downstairs and upstairs. By night, Corrie stayed in contact with the Dutch resistance movement. Soon she and her family were also hiding resistance workers wanted by the Nazis. Perhaps to return this kindness, an architect from the resistance network designed and built the hidden room. It was so well-executed, no outsider would be able to discover it. This was not a large space but it was completely safe, even if the house were searched.

Equipped with an air vent, the room's only entrance was a sliding hatch. The Nazis never found it, even when they tapped on its walls. This small space was called *De Bege*, or "the hiding place." It seemed an answer to Corrie's private prayer, offered in 1942: "Lord Jesus, I offer myself for your people. In any way. Any place. Any time." The place was here, the time was now—and Corrie was there to fulfill her offer to Christ. No one in her family seems to have shared their pastor's sense of impending disaster.

Fortunately, her connections in Haarlem were widespread and long-standing. She had created several clubs for girls and was active at the family's Dutch Reformed Church. There she had organized a special club for disabled and mentally challenged children. The Nazis had banned this group when Holland was invaded in 1940. They dismissed the handicapped as "life unworthy of life." One disabled child's father, a civil servant, remembered Corrie's kindness long after the club was disbanded. He had come to her mind as she wondered how to feed the many hungry people in her house.

The civil servant now ran the ration-card office in Haarlem. One evening, before curfew, Corrie appeared at his house. The civil servant did not appear to be surprised—nor did he ask her why she had come. His only question was: "How many ration cards do you need?" Food was scarce; her household was overflowing. "I opened my mouth to say, 'Five,'" she later wrote. "But the number that unexpectedly and astonishingly came out instead was, 'one hundred.'"

Without question, she was given the cards. She would have to use them sparingly, she knew, or she would be found out. No one had a household as big as hers was now. The civil servant kept her secret.

The ten Boom family continued its mission, acting in accordance with the Gospel. Corrie was active in the constantly changing household, defying the Nazis' law for the sake of Christ's mandate: "I was a stranger and you took me in...when you do this to the least of these, you do it to me" (see Matthew 25). They were careful and "the hiding place" was secure.

"There is no panic in heaven! God has no problems, only plans," Corrie wrote later. For nearly two years, true to conscience, the ten Boom family was deeply involved in the Haarlem resistance movement. With the help of this network, the family had rescued about eight hundred people by the early winter of 1944.

In addition to the secret room, there was a buzzer system to warn the household when suspicious strangers entered the premises. The ten Booms also held drills, timing the flight of all guests from the dining table to "the hiding place," where they would stay until the potential danger had passed. Corrie, Betsie, and their father managed to run the watch shop and keep their secret mission going.

Inevitably, however, the ten Booms' work was discovered by the Gestapo. It is thought that an apprentice in the watch shop inadvertently revealed the secret while he was on a courier run for the resistance in January 1944. Other sources ascribe the betrayal to a Dutch informer for the Nazis. It is most likely that an informer was the culprit, pretending to seek shelter for his wife.

On February 28, Corrie was in bed with fever and influenza. Suddenly, she saw the household's six "guests" dash past her into the secret room. Rising, she joined her father and her sister downstairs. There the Gestapo was already questioning them. Around the dining room table, the interrogation went on for hours. The Gestapo officers searched the premises but never found the secret room. Its occupants remained safe and, with the help of the resistance, they escaped a few days later.

There was no escaping for their hosts, however. The ten Booms were thrust into a wagon while their neighbors looked on. It is

The ten Boom family

reported that at the station house, Caspar ten Boom presented his daily Bible reading, as he had done at bedtime for decades. The family was then deported to Scheveningen prison in the Hague, the capital of Holland.

There they were sent to different quarters. About a week later, the family's eighty-four year-old patriarch fell ill and died, untreated, lying on a cot in the infirmary's hallway.

Corrie and Betsie were sent into separate solitary confinement cells where Corrie managed to get hold of a smuggled Bible. This provided some consolation, along with a hidden note from her sister, Nollie, which read: "All the watches in your closet are safe."

By train, Corrie and Betsie were transferred to the most dreaded concentration camp in Germany: Ravensbrück. There they were held as "political prisoners," grateful for each other's company in what was surely a living hell. The sisters existed on meager rations, fought off rats, and awakened at four-thirty every morning for a day of manual labor.

Betsie, born with anemia, began to grow weaker. Even so, she inspired Corrie, who struggled with her own rage at their betrayer. "No hate, no hate," Betsie cautioned. "No one who hates can walk

with God." Corrie, knowing her sister spoke the truth, finally overcame her anger.

Soon both sisters were ministering to the women of the camp.
Later, Corrie was to see this time at Ravensbrück as "their finest
hour." Betsie, meanwhile, viewed their internment in terms of the
Gospel. "This is the best way to spend the rest of our lives," she said,
showing her deep faith.

Using Corrie's smuggled Bible, the ten Boom sisters began
to hold secret worship services in the evenings. "At first," Corrie
wrote, "Betsie and I called these meetings with great timidity. But
as night after night went by and no guard ever came near us, we
grew bolder. So many now wanted to join us that we held a secret
service after evening roll call...." The two women gathered their
unofficial congregation in the dim "knitting room," used only by
day. Despite the poor lighting, the moldy walls, and the rustle of
rats, something extraordinary began to happen at these evenings
of worship and sharing.

"[These] were services like no others, these times in Barracks
28," Corrie later wrote. "A single meeting night might include a
recital of the Magnificat in Latin by a group of Roman Catholics,
a whispered hymn by some Lutherans, and a *sotto-voce* chant by
Eastern Orthodox women.

With each moment, the crowd around us would swell, packing
the nearby platforms, hanging over the edges, until the high struc-
tures groaned and swayed.

"At last either Betsie or I would open the Bible," she went on.
"Because only the Hollanders could understand the Dutch text,
we would translate aloud in German. And then we would hear the
life-giving words passed back along the aisles in French, Polish,
Russian, Czech, and back into Dutch. They were little previews of
heaven, these evenings beneath the light bulb."

After a few months, however, Betsie's health broke down entirely. While she lay in an infirmary bed, Corrie would wipe frost from the window every day so the sisters could wave at each other. As Betsie began to slip away, Corrie was allowed to visit at her bedside. "...[We] must tell them what we have learned here," Betsie whispered to her sister. "We must tell them that there is no pit so deep that He is not deeper still. They will listen to us, Corrie, because we have been here."

This inspiration from the dying Betsie ten Boom marks a pivotal point in Corrie's life. Her struggle is internal; her hatred of her tormentors has grown. It is Betsie's words that challenge Corrie to a new state of faith—the daring to act on Christ's mandate: "Love your enemies." The ten Boom family did not show any hesitation about joining the resistance movement or offering their home as a hiding place for people who came to them for help.

For Corrie, the greatest challenge of her life came at Ravensbrück, where her sister helped her turn from hatred to forgiveness. Here, too, Betsie gave Corrie her life's mission—and Corrie was able to accept it and live it out.

Betsie's words stayed with Corrie. They gave her a reason to live and a mission for the future. When Betsie died on December 16, 1944, Corrie was astonished at how peaceful and beautiful she looked; all the lines in her face had melted away, and to her sister, Betsie seemed to prefigure a heavenly state of grace.

Before the month was over, Corrie received a shock—the sudden news that she was to be released from Ravensbrück. Later she learned that a clerical error had caused her liberation. Corrie also discovered that the week after her departure, female political prisoners in her age range (over fifty) were all gassed. On Christmas Day, the massive gates of Ravensbrück opened and Corrie ten Boom walked out into freedom. "God does not have problems. Only plans," she commented.

Corrie, weakened by her ordeal, took a train to Berlin. With assistance, she transferred to another train heading for Holland. She had received one ration of bread before she left the camp, but this was lost.

Corrie was weak and suffering from starvation when she entered Holland. There, in Groningen Hospital, she was cared for until she recovered her physical strength.

Her journey back to Haarlem must have been an emotional one, especially when she reached her father's empty house; intact, but empty.

Corrie walked the narrow lanes beside Haarlem's canals and tried to acclimate herself to her new life. Lonely and disoriented, she could not even find the ten Booms' cat. Finally, Betsie's words came back to her: "We must tell them what we have learned here. We must tell them that there is no pit so deep that he is not deeper still...."

After the Allied forces liberated Holland, Corrie began this mission. Following World War II, she traveled to more than sixty countries with her message of God's love and a special emphasis on forgiveness.

Corrie was able to draw on her own struggles to express the need for reconciliation and she told colorful stories about the ten Boom Sisters' "finest hour." She also wrote several faith-based books, including *The Hiding Place*, published in 1971 and filmed in 1975. Both have enjoyed great success.

In addition to speaking and writing, Corrie founded a special home for the Holocaust survivors whose lives were in a state of extreme dislocation. Then she took a highly unusual step. She decided to establish a home for Dutch people who had collaborated with the Germans during Holland's occupation.

Her move must have grown out of Corrie's own struggle to forgive her family's betrayer. This place of hospitality also must have evoked considerable controversy. Corrie published an article in *Guideposts Magazine:* "I'm Still Learning to Forgive." As early as 1947, she had made great progress in reaching this spiritual goal and wished to help others learn as she had.

Corrie ten Boom began to travel in Germany with the message of God's love and the need for forgiveness. This belief was tested in Munich after she had just delivered a lecture. As the members of her audience began to leave. Corrie spied a man she recognized. He was working his way toward her. Despite his civilian clothes, Corrie was certain this man had been a guard at Ravensbrück. She remembered him in uniform; she remembered arriving at the camp with a group of women; they were forced to shed their clothes while he had looked on. Now the man kept drawing closer. Could she actually put her own words into practice and forgive him? She did not know.

In Corrie's book, *The Hiding Place*, she describes this meeting. "'You mentioned Ravensbrück in your talk,' he said. 'I was a guard in there...but since that time I have become a Christian. I know that God has forgiven me for the cruel things I did there, but I would like to hear it from your lips as well. *Fraulein...*' His hand came out...'Will you forgive me?' And I stood there...and I could not do it," Corrie admits. "'Jesus, help me!' I prayed silently. 'I can lift my hand, I can do that much. You supply the feeling,'" she told God. This would have to be a supreme act of will; a spiritual challenge Corrie never expected.

"And so, woodenly, mechanically," she went on, "I thrust my hand into the one stretched out to me. And as I did, an incredible thing took place. The current started in my shoulder, raced down my arm, and sprang into our joined hands. And then this feeling of warmth seemed to flood my whole being, bringing tears to my eyes. 'I forgive you, brother!' I cried. 'With all my heart!' For a long moment we grasped each other's hands, the former guard and the former prisoner. I had never known God's love so intensely as I did then."

Corrie continued with her reconciling work until she was eighty-five, when a series of strokes made travel impossible for her. Before her illness, Corrie was knighted by the queen of the Netherlands. Israel also honored her as one of the Righteous Among the Nations.

Corrie ten Boom spent her last years in Orange, California, where she died on her ninety-first birthday. Today, *The Hiding Place* is still read and the ten Boom home in Haarlem has become a monument to that courageous family. Now a museum, it is visited by thousands each year. People worldwide remain drawn to this center of enacted courage and conscience that presents inspiration—and a challenge—to its visitors.

....

Questions for Reflection and Discussion

1. How would you define Corrie and Betsie ten Boom's example?
2. What sustained them more than anything?
3. Were they motivated by faith—or anger?
   Could they have been motivated by both?
4. Why did the ten Booms' neighbors refrain from following their example?
5. How did Betsie inspire Corrie?
6. Do you think the sisters were "driven" or "called?"
7. What can these sisters' lives teach us in our time?
8. Can we live up to the ten Booms' commitment today?
9. Would you have taken the ten Booms' risk?
10. What are the "moments of truth" for these heroines?

María de la Luz Camacho
of Mexico City
(1907–1934)

The news was bad. In their black-and-red uniforms, angry youths were massing in the park across from the parish church of Coyoacán in Mexico. Other sanctuaries had been burned to the ground in recent years; a Communist movement, the Red Syndicate, had declared war on Mexican Catholicism.

When this news reached María de la Luz Camacho, she opened the armoire in her bedroom and selected her best clothing. With care, she pulled the fine dress over her head and let its folds fall into place around her. Her family asked María why she was so specially arrayed. It was, after all, an ordinary day; New Year's Eve was forty-eight hours away.

María smiled. "We are going to defend Christ, our king," she explained. She could not then know what such a defense would cost. By the time she reached her church, María saw about sixty young men drinking, shouting, and threatening to torch the sanctuary. María knew they were fully capable of such an action, especially as their numbers grew and their intoxication increased. For two years now, Mexican Catholics had lived in fear of the "Red Shirts." They had closed down churches they did not burn so that secret Masses had to be said in private homes. Priests were arrested or attacked; some moved about their parishioners in disguise.

Catholic Action, a small network, tried to counter the Communists; María had joined this resistance movement. At twenty-seven, she understood the situation she was about to confront in her festival dress.

She also knew that hundreds of children were at Mass inside the church. María de la Luz Camacho positioned herself before the sanctuary's doors. Her sister and a handful of other young women joined her. Even so, their numbers could not compare with the mob before them. Behind the church doors were children María knew well.

Because priests were now few, selected lay people became catechists; María had been one for a dozen years. She was also a lay member of the Order of Saint Francis, offering support to the Franciscan Friars. María's dedication to her faith had a long history of commitment. After turning down a number of marriage proposals, she had told her father that she wished to enter a convent but did not want to cause him the expense of her dowry.

She understood the challenges of religious life: "It is the anvil on which God hammers his saints into shape with the hammer of sacrifice." Now, however, María was not thinking of the cloister's safety. She only hoped to hold off the mob until the children could escape the church through a back door, where a priest would lead them to safety.

Many of these endangered children had crowded into her home on Saturday nights, where she had instructed them in doctrine and in prayer. A young man slipped away from the mob and approached María, urging her to flee for her life. She remembered him as one of her catechumens.

Saddened to see him with the "Red Shirts," she surveyed the crowd. She could have fled the scene and chosen safety. Perhaps she hesitated, caught in this dilemma. This was her watershed moment. In the end, she made a costly choice: she refused to leave the church steps.

The mob began to taunt her, shouting "God is dead!" In answer, María called back, *"Viva Christo rey,"* or "Long live Christ the king." This was the rallying cry of the Catholic Action Movement. For some time, the mob and the women exchanged hostile words. Meanwhile, María hoped, the children were slipping away from danger.

The mob ordered María and her small band of women to move away from the church doors. As the group's spokesperson, María shouted back to the young men, "We are not afraid. If it becomes necessary, we are ready to die for Christ the king. Those who wish to enter this church must first pass over my body." The mob jeered, gaining strength and bravado from one another—as mobs always have. "There is no God," they taunted the women. "Long live the revolution," shouted the mob. Again, María and her friends responded with their movement's watchwords: *"Viva Christo rey."*

Had María de la Luz Camacho always known, somehow, that she would come to this place, this time, this dangerous stand? Perhaps she did. A friend once questioned her about her willingness to stand on principle—at all costs. "What would you do if you had to choose between losing your faith to be happy in this world, or living in the other world by dying to preserve your faith?" María did not take long to respond with confidence: "God would give me the grace to be faithful to him. Besides, if I had the misfortune to deny my God, I should die of grief." Clearly, this life-or-death dilemma had been on her mind and in her heart.

Her name means "María of the light," a popular title for the Virgin Mary in Mexico. Born in Mexico City on May 17, 1907, there was little indication that she would find herself defending her faith twenty-seven years later. Her father, Manuel Camacho, was a well-to-do businessman.

After her mother's early death, the household underwent a time of turbulence. The young María reacted with tantrums and obstinate behavior. After every outburst, however, she always asked for forgiveness—only to explode with fury again. However, her father eventually married a fine and devout woman, and the Camacho home became a stable and happy one.

Perhaps inspired by her stepmother, María grew up with a strong devotion to her faith. But the peacefulness of her childhood gave way to an upheaval in Mexico. Legal sanctions were passed to eradicate the Catholic faith, and Communist insurgents launched a lasting attack on the Church. Throughout these turbulent times, María worked among the city's poor, distributing food and clothing. In the evenings, she taught secret catechism classes and also tutored children in reading; literacy, as well as faith, was important to her.

María de la Luz was certainly devout—but she was not prudish. A natural musician, she played the violin and also wrote plays, first for her siblings, then for the people of Coyoacán, where her family now lived. Biographer Joan Carroll Cruz describes María as "a lighthearted person who often sang as she went about her chores. She also had an outgoing personality, and was often impetuous and high-spirited."

Was her stand before the church just another example of María's impetuous nature? Was she casting herself as the leading lady in the most dramatic role she could craft as an amateur playwright? María's stand for conscience could indeed be interpreted that way. In weighing what we know of her, however, I see a different motivation.

María had matured and showed consideration of others, including her father. She had delayed her entry into a convent so that she could pay her dowry herself. In addition, the work she did was neither glamorous nor glorious.

The slums of Mexico City held little allure for most young women, and María, from a comfortable family, could have easily married into even greater wealth. But her consistent commitment to the Franciscan Order and the Catholic Action Movement showed a steadfast and humble devotion to her faith. There was nothing self-aggrandizing about her daily activities, year after year. Her choice to teach catechism in a beleaguered church also seems to bear out the sincerity of her calling.

Sometimes, María was the subject of gossip and envy. She must have seemed to have it all, from material blessings to spiritual devotion. She confessed to her spiritual director that she suffered "interior trials" from time to time and she was often hard on herself. Under her high-spirited facade lay a serious, perhaps overly scrupulous woman of faith.

Gradually, she adjusted to the fact that people would not always understand her. "I do good and let people talk," she confided to her spiritual director. "When one can bear the pain alone, why make others suffer?" This perspective, again, seems to indicate maturity. At the time of María's stand before her parish church, she was helping out at home and working to earn money for the dowry to present to the convent.

One wonders what could have run through her mind as she continued to hold off the mob, that late December morning. Perhaps she thought again of the cloister. But perhaps she only thought of the crisis she confronted. Perhaps she thought she would simply delay the angry crowd until she knew the children had safely escaped the church. Perhaps she thought she could dissuade the men who were swigging cognac to arouse their courage. They must have looked so young to her; so many had been her students. They were also a mob, and as María stood there, she must have decided to risk their retribution.

And now, María could see the men were armed. She did not move. Until the children were safe, all she could do was continue to exchange verbal fire with the crowd.

No one knows exactly how long the standoff continued. The mob, rather than dispersing, must have reached a critical mass, as well as a critical level of intoxication and intolerance. In a culture that prized machismo, how could strong, swaggering young men allow themselves to be taunted—even insulted—by a handful of women?

The level of frustration, humiliation, and anger spun out of control and finally, in moments, the standoff ended. Shots rang out. María de la Luz was struck in the chest and fell backward. Her best dress was covered in blood. Fatally wounded, she did not linger long. Surrounded by her small group of women, she died on the church steps.

When it was clear to the crowd that this young woman was dead, the "Red Shirts" seemed to react with shock and fear. The mob shifted again, this time away from whoever had done the shooting. The young men murmured among themselves and slowly dispersed. María's sister cradled the lifeless body in the festival clothes. Meanwhile, the children had safely escaped from the church, along with the priest, and the mob's plans to burn down the building were thwarted. Hundreds of lives had been saved, as well as the treasured sanctuary.

Perhaps some of María's former students felt their comrades had gone too far. Perhaps they were not the only ones who had not intended this turn of events. Whatever their thoughts, the young men swiftly distanced themselves from the tragic incident. Some might have seen María's death as a waste of talent and passion: gone was the playwright, the violinist, the potential nun. Most, however, saw her death differently, as evidenced by the outpouring of emotion that followed.

The martyr's body was carried to her family's home. It is estimated that some two thousand mourners filed past her coffin, leaving small tokens of love and respect. María's wake continued until dawn, and during the night a priest arrived to place palms around the heroine's body. The priest reminded the mourners to see María's death in terms of the resurrection.

After María's funeral Mass, some thirty thousand people accompanied the cortege to the cemetery in Xoco. The sight must have been impressive and moving: a strong signal sent by the resistance to its oppressors. The casket was escorted by white-clad women and children carrying palms, and by men of the Catholic Action Movement. Everyone in the procession sang hymns and chanted prayers as the line of mourners wound toward the grave site. Palms waved. Voices rose. Shoes and boots tramped on along the route.

Newspapers gave the event wide coverage, triggering protests against the Communist radicals. Mexico's president was contacted by telegram. The country's archbishop, D. Pascal Diaz Barretto, marched with the other mourners. It is reported that he was deeply moved by the sight of so many people honoring María de la Luz Camacho and moving in public without any thought of government reprisals.

"God would give me the grace to be faithful to him," María had told her friend. "Besides, if I had the misfortune to deny my God, I should die of grief." María de la Luz Camacho no longer had to dread dying of grief.

Her death was considered glorious and courageous, giving the people of Mexico a rallying point for their continued struggle against oppression.

Today, María's name is included on the roll-call of Mexican patriots and Christian martyrs. The Catholic Church has accepted her cause for beatification, the first step toward canonization as a saint. Her life is best summed up in her own words: denying her beliefs would be far worse than death.

Questions for Reflection and Discussion

1. How would you evaluate María's stand for conscience?
2. What sustained her more than anything?
3. Was she motivated by faith—or anger?
   Could she have been motivated by both?
4. Did she waste her gifts by taking a stand?
5. Was María's "mission" egocentric or heroic?
6. Do you think she was "deluded" or "called?"
7. What can María de la Luz's life teach us in our time?
8. Was María fanatic or faithful?
9. Would you have taken María's stand?
10. Where is "the moment of truth" for this heroine?

SECTION TWO

Daughters of Determination

FOR ALL THE SAINTS WHO LIVED BESIDE US
WHOSE WEAKNESSES AND STRENGTHS
WERE WOVEN WITH OUR OWN,
WE PRAISE YOU, O GOD.

Anne Askew of London
(1521-1546)

The burning of Anne Askew at Smithfield, England, July 16, 1546.

Names. It was names they wanted. Who was with you? Who are your comrades in heresy? Who lured you to London? Who made you preach in the streets, making a show of yourself—you, a married woman? Give us their names, these Gospelers, or it will go hard for you.

The questioning seemed endless. Anne Askew regarded her captors in silence. Anything she said would bring trouble on her friends. Trouble, in 1546, could take a sudden, drastic turn. The times themselves were troubled.

Henry VIII was a capricious monarch. And even he had imprisoned his old friend and former chancellor, Thomas More, where Anne stood now: the infamous Tower of London. After breaking with the Catholic Church, he still persecuted Protestants more radical than he. Their severed heads were stuck on spikes for all to see.

Mistress Askew was well aware of what happened to those who disagreed with the king. After a year in prison, More was beheaded here. Henry's Protestant queen, Anne Boleyn, was executed in the same way. Even children knew what happened to people sent to this ancient fortress. It was imposing. It was grim. It was feared.

How had Anne Askew come to stand here, before the king's inquisitors, within the tower's dank walls? She must have asked herself that question more than once. This was not the outcome she had foreseen when she was growing up, wandering the beautiful green lands of Lincolnshire. Her hope, then, was to be a Protestant devotional poet. Of course she must sign her work with a man's name, but writing was one of Anne's great loves.

Even greater, however, was her religious faith. Educated, privileged, devout, the daughter of an aristocratic family, Anne was not likely to be endangered by anyone. Surely, she would say her prayers by the fire, write her poems, and walk this countryside for the rest of her life.

Perhaps she contemplated a life of prayer. Her nature was artistic and religious. At fifteen years old, however, Anne was endangered—by her own father, Sir William Askew. He could not be dissuaded once he made a seemingly sudden decision: Anne must wed Thomas Kyme, who had been engaged to her late sister, Martha. Kyme must have presented a lucrative offer to Sir William, one that must not slip away. And why would a patriarch heed his young daughter on such a crucial matter? After a brief mourning period for Martha, Anne was forced to marry Thomas Kyme, about whom little is known. One may conclude that the match was advantageous for everyone—except the bride.

From the beginning, the union was unhappy. Kyme objected to Anne's religious commitment and long times of prayer. Anne responded with defiance, escaping to London, where she soon found friends among like-minded Protestants. Her humiliated husband was called to bring her home, but as soon as she arrived, he locked Anne out of the house. The sources are unclear as to whether this marriage produced two children; if it did, nothing is known about them. This much is known: Anne, breaking with age-old tradition, refused to take her husband's name.

In time, Anne escaped again to London, where she sought a divorce. Such an initiative, undertaken by a woman of her times, would have been unusual, at the very least. Anne claimed scriptural warrant from 1 Corinthians 7:15, which allowed divorce if a spouse was an unbeliever. Once more, her husband was summoned to take her home and put her in her place. Once again, Anne defied him, vanishing from his household forever.

She returned to her devout Protestant comrades in London, where she found a more congenial atmosphere. One wonders at her mobility in such an era. She must have been an excellent horsewoman, unafraid of traveling alone, and in possession of strong of will. She would soon need all the spirit and strength she had to draw upon.

In London, Anne's religious devotion increased, encouraged by her comrades. With them, she read banned Protestant books and soon began to distribute them. Her commitment to her faith remained firm, and she must have felt she was obeying God's will when she repeatedly broke the law of the land.

In addition, she began to preach about the Protestant faith, trying to explain her understanding of its sacramental theology. The sincerity of Anne's voice, as it comes down to us in her own writings, does not show a headstrong spirit but a reasonable one. Reason, however, did not always rule Tudor England, nor did dissent.

Inevitably, Anne Askew was arrested for the possession and distribution of banned books, "heretical" in nature, and perhaps for disturbing the peace with her preaching. Such an act, if done in public, would have been considered lewd, unseemly, and unscriptural for a woman.

In addition, it was then illegal for a woman to possess a Bible. Under arrest and intense interrogation, Anne Askew must have reached her own "tipping point." She made some internal decision which, she knew, would lead her into grave danger. If she abjured her beliefs and gave up the names of her comrades, Anne might escape dire consequences. If she dared to stand on principle, resist all pressure, and name no names, she knew she would suffer.

At some point during her interrogations, she made the toughest choice of her life. She would take the second way. She would remain openly true to her beliefs. And she would give up no names. Anne Askew defied the expectations and demands of others—and became the only woman to be tortured in the Tower of London.

Sir Anthony Kingston, the constable of the tower, was given his orders. He was commanded to torture Anne Askew unless she divulged the names of other Protestants with whom she had consorted; from whom she had acquired books; and by whose authority or encouragement she had the temerity to preach. Anne Askew refused to give up a single comrade's name. Her infuriated interrogators threatened and pleaded.

Anne stood firm in her loyalty, answering her questioners with wit and spirit. Growing desperate, Anne's inquisitors asked her whether she received God by consuming a consecrated wafer, her only answer was a smile. And then the questioning came back to its central purpose: The naming of names. The betrayal of trust. The cave-in of loyalty for one's own salvation. The compromise with one's conscience. On these matters, Askew did not budge.

This issue of loyalty under duress is not lost in distant English history. The question recurred in the middle of the last century in the United States of America during what is still known informally as the "McCarthy Era." In the 1950s, in what was termed a "witch hunt," Senator Joseph McCarthy and others pressured witnesses before his committee to declare if they were or ever had been Communists. In addition, they were put under great duress to give up names of Communists they knew about. If they failed to comply, these witnesses were blacklisted; no one would hire them for work.

In Anne Askew's day, the penalty was even more severe: assignment to the most dreaded torture instrument—the rack. This diabolical contraption stretched the human frame so that joints, sinews, and muscles were pulled apart, inducing agony in the victim. In addition, the rack had such a strong effect on wrists that blood spurted out from underneath the fingernails. Strong men had informed on others rather than be subjected to this extreme form of torture.

Anne, a twenty-four-year-old woman, was taken to a chamber in "the White Tower," where she was asked again for the names of fellow believers. She kept silent as she regarded the torture machine. Then she was stripped to her shift and spread out on the rack. Once more, she was asked for the names of her Protestant comrades. Once more, she said nothing—but this time she did not smile.

According to her own writings and to John Foxe's *Book of Martyrs*, Sir Anthony Kingston and an assistant turned the rack's wheel, causing Anne to be raised up and held spread out in the air above the rack itself. In her account of her ordeal, written from her tower cell, she admitted that the pain caused her to faint. After she was lowered, she regained consciousness and the same form of torture was administered twice more, with the same results. Anne, no doubt, had neared her breaking point.

Even so, she still spoke no word and gave no names. Finally, Kingston ordered the torture suspended while he went to confer with King Henry. Begging the king's pardon, Kingston admitted that he could not continue. He was excused, but the torture continued.

Richard Rich, betrayer of Thomas More, took over the torture, with the aid of one Thomas Wriothesley. They employed the ratchet as well as the wheel, intensifying the stretching of the human form, without respite. Anne cried out then, though she still spoke no words. Richard Rich was merciless. He continued the racking with the ratchet and was impervious to his victim's agony.

Anne's cries grew so loud and so anguished, an official's wife and daughter, walking in a nearby garden, rushed inside and shut their windows. Bleeding from her fingernails and broken in body, Anne was finally returned to her cell in silence. Anne protected her friends and never uttered even one of their names.

In her cell, Anne Askew set down her experiences in the tower and wrote of her religious beliefs, although this work was not published under her own name. It must have seemed long ago that she had contemplated publishing her poetry this way; now she was publishing autobiography and religious witness. Her account was brought out as *The Examinations of John Bale,* and another account was printed in 1563 in Foxe's *Book of Martyrs.*

From the Tower of London, the imprisoned "heretic" wrote a sincere and surprisingly calm letter to her sovereign. In it she desires to clarify her beliefs and asks—but does not beg—for the king's mercy.

And yet, she still held back what Henry wanted from her: names. She wrote: "I, Anne Askew, to whom God has given to me the bread of adversity and the water of trouble (yet not so much as my sins deserved), desire to make known this matter unto your Grace.

"For inasmuch as I am by the law condemned for an evildoer, I here take heaven and earth to record that I shall die in my innocence.

"According to what I have said first and will say to the last, I utterly abhor and detest all heresies, but concerning the Supper of the Lord, I believe just what Christ has said within the Holy Scriptures, which He also confirmed with His own blessed blood. I believe that He has willed me to follow Him, and I believe all that the true Church does teach concerning Him.

"For I will not forsake the commandment of His Holy Words, for what the Lord has charged me by His Word, I keep in my heart. I, therefore, most humbly beg your Grace to look kindly on my unfortunate circumstances.

"Your most obedient and humble servant, Anne Askew."

Anne's religious convictions held up under pressure. "O Lord," she wrote in prayer, "I have more enemies now than there be hairs on my head. Yet, Lord, let them never overcome me with vain words but fight Thou, Lord, in my stead: for on Thee I cast my care." There was still time for her to save her life by naming her comrades. Anne Askew did not avail herself of this opportunity. One wonders what could have sustained her.

Certainly Anne seems strong-willed, but that does not seem to explain her silence. The only other explanation is the strength of her faith. She would not deny her Lord, like Peter, nor would she betray a comrade, as did Judas. Perhaps she recalled the words of Jesus: "Greater love has no man but this, that he lay down his life for his friends."

The silence in her cell was nearly complete, except for the scratching of Anne's quill on paper. Following the example of Christ on the cross, she penned these words: "Lord, I heartily desire of Thee, that Thou wilt of Thy merciful goodness forgive them that violence which they do and have done unto me. So be it, Lord."

She was sent up for a perfunctory courtroom trial. The jury might have taken pity on Anne; she was so severely injured by her torture, she could no longer walk; instead, she was carried into the courtroom tied onto a chair.

However, it would seem that no juror had her scruples. The rack's terror was confirmed for them by the very sight of Askew, and the jury's verdict went against her. The charge was universally dreaded: heresy. The sentence, pronounced by the judge, was no surprise: Anne was to be burned at the stake.

At this juncture, Sir William Askew might have visited London to bid his daughter farewell—or intervene on her behalf. Her father, however, was careful of his own welfare. Anne awaited her death alone. One wonders if she experienced any regrets over her defiant life.

Had she wasted her gifts and abilities for a religious belief? Had she sacrificed her talents as a poet for some stubborn adherence to her code of loyalty? From her writings, no such regrets nagged at her as she set down her account of life. She had followed her conscience and her God. When a priest appeared to hear her last confession, she declined his offer.

On July 16, 1546, again confined to a chair, Anne Askew was carried under guard to Smithfield, London. Eyewitness sources note that she was dragged from her chair to the stake, which had a seat built in for her. Three men, burned with her, were forced to stand. Before the fatal fire was kindled, Anne was asked once more if she would repent of her heresy, recant of her beliefs, or reveal her comrades' names. She did not give in to any of these demands. Her only response was to the traditional plea for pardon from the executioner. This she gave as a man doused her with gunpowder, to shorten her ordeal.

The king's current wife, Lady Jane Grey, was one of the witnesses to this execution. She and others noted Anne's bravery as she was tied to the stake and the fire was lit. She had faced torture alone; now, loyal to God and friends, she faced death in the same way. It was reported that Anne Askew did not cry out as her clothes began to burn and only screamed "when the flames reached her chest." One hopes that the gunpowder was quick to explode and accelerate the process.

John Foxe, in his *Acts and Monuments*, noted that Anne Askew left behind her "a singular example of Christian constancy for all men to follow." Anne's final words were the repetition of a prayer she composed shortly before her death:

> "To Thee, O Lord, I bequeath my spirit,
> Which art the work master of the same.
> It is thine, Lord: therefore, take it of right,
> My body on earth I leave, from whence it came.
> Although to ashes it be now burned,
> I know Thou can'st raise it again
> In the same likeness that Thou it formed,
> In heaven with Thee evermore to remain."
>
> ~ANNE ASKEW, 1546

....

Questions for Reflection and Discussion

1. How would you define Anne Askew's example?
2. What sustained her more than anything?
3. Was she motivated by faith or rebellion?
   Could she have been motivated by both?
4. Would you have given names of friends to keep yourself from torture?
5. Was Anne's "mission" egocentric or heroic?
6. Do you think she was "wild" or "called?"
   Could she have been both?
7. What can Anne's life teach us about loyalty?
8. Do we need Anne's kind of commitment today?
9. Would you have stayed "safe" or gone to London, as Anne did?
10. Where is "the moment of truth" for this heroine?

Rebecca Nurse of Salem (1621–1692)

Trial of two "witches," Salem, Massachusetts, 1692

"Witch!" Fingers pointed. Voices rose. Amid the tumult of the courtroom, the white-haired woman stood still, dignified, and calm.

"How can you stand so?" the judge demanded of Rebecca Nurse. "You do not know my heart," she said quietly. She was right. "Confess and save your life," Judge John Hathorne urged her. Rebecca must have looked at him in wonder as she spoke: "Would you have me belie myself?"

Others had already done so; more would. This was the only way to escape the noose during that tragic and turbulent year of 1692, when witchcraft hysteria took over Salem Village in Massachusetts. More than a hundred of its citizens were accused of this crime: a hanging offense, based on the Prophet Samuel's injunction: "Thou shalt not suffer a witch to live." The persecution of women as witches had a long history in Europe before it reached Massachusetts Bay's oldest settlement, named after the Hebrew word for peace: Shalom.

Founded in 1621, Salem was chartered in the year of Rebecca's birth. Another irony was her mother's maiden name. Rebecca was born to Joanna Blessing and William Towne of Yarmouth, England. This Puritan family emigrated to Salem about 1640, as England plunged into civil war.

It was in Salem, five years later, that Rebecca Towne married Francis Nurse, an artisan who worked in wood. Highly respected for his craft, Francis became the town's official constable for a time. For fifty years, he lived in Salem Village with an unimpeachable reputation.

His wife was also widely admired. The mother of eight children, she was well-known for her great kindness, her deep piety, and her expert midwifery. Beloved of all, Goodwife Nurse was an exemplar of gentle faith when, at seventy-one, she was arrested on charges of witchcraft. It is said that Salem's magistrates were reluctant to present her with an arrest warrant. Nurse was not entirely surprised. She had heard that she was considered a suspect. Her reaction is reported in these words: "I am innocent as the child unborn, but surely, what sin hath God found out in me...that he should lay such an affliction on me in my old age?"

Her accusers were the Putnams, whose land bordered on the Nurses' property. There had been a boundary dispute between the two families; the issue's resolution favored Francis Nurse. The Putnams, lacking their neighbor's pasture lands and prestige, held a long-standing grudge. It cannot be mere coincidence that the Putnams' young daughter, Ann, the first of four girls to "cry witch," singled out Rebecca.

Historians have conjectured that the Putnams stood to gain if their neighbor's lands were confiscated. This supposition cannot be proved; however, it is buttressed by Ann's remorse, set down in writing in 1706.

There was no remorse evident in 1692, however. Ann claimed that she saw Goodwife Nurse's spirit tormenting her at night.

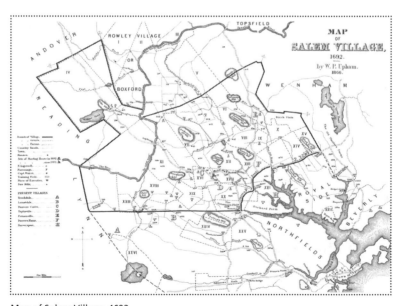

Map of Salem Village, 1692

Ann's mother added her own accusation: Rebecca had served as her midwife four times, and each newborn had died. In the midst of the town's hysteria, these claims were taken seriously enough to warrant an arrest.

This action so shocked the town, thirty-nine citizens signed a petition of protest: a brave act in a time of great fear. Nonetheless, Rebecca Nurse was carted away from her home and locked up with other suspects in Salem's overflowing jail.

With grace and poise, she held her ground, while others began to offer false admissions of guilt. Goodwife Hobbs was released from imprisonment after this confession: She had tormented girls by order of Satan and flew through the air to a witches' conventicle.

Hobbs's statements set an unfortunate precedent, even as more citizens were arrested. Other jails were filled and sources affirm that "the colony teetered on the brink of chaos." Governor William Phips took decisive action, setting up a special court to hear the multiplying witchcraft cases.

His choice for the court's chief justice was hardly unbiased— William Stoughton, a zealous judge who saw his mission as "ridding

The house of Rebecca Nurse

the country of witches." It would seem that Rebecca Nurse understood her situation and, in prison, came to terms with her impending death. Quietly and privately, she faced her dilemma—and rejected any betrayal of her conscience. Her simple, poignant, and faith-filled commentary sums up her character, as well as her grasp of events. "I have no one to turn to but God," she declared at her trial. When asked if she had seen the devil or anyone with him, she made no confession—and gave up no names of friends of neighbors.

By contrast, several other accused villagers followed the example of Goodwife Hobbs. One notable exception was Giles Corey, an octogenarian who refused to admit to wizardry and was sentenced to be "pressed to death" by a pile of rocks. Corey, like Nurse, gave no names.

Unfortunately, this issue of betrayal for gain did not end with the Salem witchcraft hysteria. It recurred in a different context as recently as the 1950s in the United States. During the so-called "McCarthy Era," Senator Joseph McCarthy and his committee accused citizens of Communist involvement and pressured them to name others who shared their beliefs. The House Un-American Activities Committee did likewise. This episode also became a kind of hysteria, inspiring playwright Arthur Miller's classic work, *The Crucible,* set in the context of Salem's witchcraft frenzy. The play is still performed today and remains a cautionary tale. Rebecca Nurse is one of its key characters.

What caused this outbreak of hysteria in late seventeenth-century Salem (and to a lesser extent in the Massachusetts towns of Ipswich and Andover)? What is the setting for Rebecca's stand for conscience? There are several answers. One has to do with class, while another has to do with land. The accused were generally wealthier than their opponents and also supported George Burroughs, a minister evicted from his office by the "witches'" accusers.

Later theories find another contributing factor to the situation. The accusers were primarily young girls who displayed symptoms associated with demonic oppression or possession. They also ate rye cereal, which is thought to have been contaminated with a powerful mold called ergot.

Rebecca Nurse, as a midwife, would have known ergot's powerful effect in speeding up the contractions of women in labor. In fact, ergot can cause spasms, convulsions—and hallucinations. It is an ingredient in some psychedelic drugs, and its presence in the young girls' food supply could explain their vivid images of the devil leading Salem's citizens to afflict their neighbors.

Some historians blame the repressiveness of Puritan society for the "witchcraft" outbreak. However, such exemplary and pious figures as Rebecca Nurse and Giles Corey undermine this supposition. Clearly, a combination of factors created the whirlwind that took the lives of twenty people.

Rebecca's courageous stand may have inspired others and helped break the hysteria in Salem. However, it did not wane until autumn and by then, Rebecca Nurse had been executed.

Rebecca, elderly, frail, and infirm, was forced to remain in jail for nearly four months. The conditions in the jail were almost certainly poor. Overcrowding has been reported; inadequate food, ventilation, and sanitation were inevitable. Even so, Rebecca refused to give way, while scores of others did.

Rebecca was indicted on June 2, 1692, and brought to court on June 30. In the transcript of this proceeding, Rebecca Nurse shows a steadfast adherence to her convictions. The scene must have been dramatic: The packed courthouse, the screaming girls, allegedly "afflicted," the craned necks and penetrating stares.

And into this setting Rebecca Nurse slowly walks, her white hair partly covered by a cap. She has been weakened physically by imprisonment. Her spirit, however, seems strong. Perhaps her eyes sweep the courtroom for a glimpse of her husband and children. The face she sees most clearly is her neighbor's—and her enemy's. When Ann Putnam and another witness cry out, Judge Hathorne demands of Rebecca: "Goody Nurse, here...Ann Putnam and Abigail Williams complain of your hurting them. What do you say to it?" Without any noted hesitation, Nurse responds, "I can say before my eternal father I am innocent, and God will clear my innocency."

Next, one Henry Kenny steps forward. He accuses Nurse of coming into his house, whereupon he was "seized twice with an amaz'd condition." Rebecca answers this accusation clearly: "I am innocent and clear and have not been able to get out of doors these eight or nine days."

Thomas Putnam, Ann's husband, stands as a witness. Nurse, he swears, murdered his wife's infants at birth. All eyes turn to the aged midwife who states: "I have never affected no child in my life." Two more step forward with accusations and Nurse retains her grace under increasing pressure. "The Lord knows I have not hurt them," she asserts.

"I am an innocent person." At this point, Judge Hathorne turns to the defendant; his words attest to her composure. "It is very awful to all to see these agonies..." Hathorne notes. "And yet you stand with dry eyes when there are so many wet—" Here Rebecca cuts him off with her famous words, "You do not know my heart."

Hathorne presses her further: "You would do well if you are guilty to confess and give glory to God." Rebecca, unmoved, does not budge. "I am as clear as the child unborn," she tells the court. After several more similar exchanges, the "afflicted" girls break into fits of screaming and contortions. The judge pounces on Nurse. "Is it not an accountable case that when you are examined, these persons are afflicted?" Rebecca Nurse utters her faith-filled statement: "I have nobody to look to but God." The judge appears to ignore her response. More testimony is heaped against her; Nurse holds her own and refuses "to belie" herself and her conscience. As she is led away, Nurse, who is hearing impaired, does not catch a final question, and her silence was taken as assent to her guilt.

However, all positive character references and supporting evidence were not totally ignored. On June 30, after Nurse's testimony, the jury surprised the court by returning a verdict of innocence.

This ruling was greeted by a furious cry of protest from Rebecca's accusers and the courtroom lapsed into chaos. The "afflicted" girls fell to the floor with a new series of fits and screams. Banging his gavel for order, Judge Hathorne surveyed the situation. Once order was restored, the judge turned his gaze on the jury. He strongly urged its members to go out again and reconsider their decision.

Although there was precedent for this legal maneuver in seventeenth-century jurisprudence, it seems likely that Hathorne's tone was ominous. Soon the jury reentered the courtroom with a different verdict: Guilty. Rebecca was returned to prison until July 3, when she was brought into Salem's meeting house—and another large crowd.

At this point in the year, about halfway through the month of accusations, Salem's witchcraft hysteria was at its peak. In this atmosphere, Rebecca Nurse was excommunicated from her church. There were no dissenting votes.

The decree of excommunication was daunting. Read out before all, Rebecca was "severed" from the Body of Christ and declared henceforth to be a heathen, delivered up to the devil and "eternally damned." There is no record of a response from the new outcast who must have anticipated this moment and faced it with dignity.

On July 19 , at the warmest phase of a New England summer, Rebecca Nurse was helped up into a cart with three other condemned women. One of these was Sarah Goode, a homeless woman, who shouted curses at her accusers and other onlookers. This rain of curses continued as the four were assisted in mounting the platform on Gallows Hill. Rebecca approached the gallows in silence; Sarah Goode continued to rail at all in attendance. Through Goode's angry tirade, those standing close to the gibbet could hear Rebecca Nurse begin to speak the words of the Lord's Prayer.

After the execution had been carried out and its results were viewed, the four lifeless bodies were taken down from the gibbet and buried without ceremony in a common, shallow grave on Gallows Hill. These "convicted witches" could not be buried in consecrated ground.

That night, however, Rebecca's sons and grandsons returned to the infamous hill under cover of darkness. The men brought shovels and probably a wooden coffin crafted by Francis Nurse. Rebecca's body was removed from Gallows Hill and transported to her family's large homestead. There, in a secret location, Rebecca Nurse was buried while her devoted family surrounded her permanent resting place. In the background stood the commodious house where she had raised her children. It stands there still, on twenty-seven acres of the original land-grant of three hundred.

Two months after this tragedy, another befell the Nurse family. Rebecca's sister, Mary Eastey, was also hanged as a witch on Gallows Hill. However, fifteen years after Rebecca's excommunication, this sentence was revoked. Nineteen years after the July hanging, Ann Putnam issued a public apology to the Nurse family for her accusations. The Massachusetts government waited nearly twenty years to compensate Rebecca's family for "wrongful death." Ironically, a descendent of the Putnam accusers became the owner of the property in 1784 and held the title until 1908.

The house and property are now open to the public. Although several officials and jurors issued public statements of repentance for the Salem witch trials, the chief justice of the court, William Stoughton, offered no apology or excuse. Governor Phips blamed Stoughton for this black mark on the colony's history. Stoughton lashed back, still intent on witch hunting. He was elected governor of Massachusetts.

Rebecca Nurse remains a courageous example of Christian conscience under great stress. Sustained by her faith, her life has inspired numerous portrayals in plays, films, novels, and poetry. Those who visit her family home find it filled with peace and light.

Questions for Reflection and Discussion

1. How would you define Rebecca Nurse's stand?
2. What sustained her more than anything?
3. Was she motivated by faith—or confusion?
4. When does personal courage put others at risk?
5. Was Rebecca Nurse's stand obstinate or heroic?
6. Do you think she should have confessed to witchcraft and saved herself?
7. What can Rebecca Nurse's life teach us in our time?
8. Where do we need Rebecca Nurse's kind of commitment today?
9. Would you have taken Rebecca's stand?
10. Where is "the moment of truth" for this heroine?

Honora "Nano" Nagle of Cork
(1718–1784)

In the beginning, they gathered in a dim, mud-walled hut. Voices were lowered. A lookout was posted. There were no windows—which was just as well. These were illegal meetings. Their leader, a small woman, lifted the lantern in her hand. As always, she opened each session with certain prayers—also illegal. The penalties for her activities were harsh: imprisonment or death.

Honora Nagle was not afraid. As a child, she had studied out-doors in secret "hedge schools" run by itinerant schoolmasters or courageous priests. Now, in 1749, "Nano" Nagle was the one who dared to teach Irish Catholic children, defying the British Penal Codes imposed on her people.

As long as she could remember, these strict laws had existed. The ruling British government forbade the Catholic religion, Catholic education, the Irish language, Irish culture, even Irish music. Irish Catholics could not own land, vote, or hold political office. Even green, the national color, was prohibited for use in clothing. The emblems of Irish Catholic Republicanism, the harp and the sham-rock, were banned and burned.

Nano's people longed for liberation; meanwhile, they were always looking for ways to preserve their faith, tradition, and civil rights. These traditions were at the core of their identity, their sense of self, their Irishness. Despite the scorn of their British conquerors, Irish Catholics passed down these traditions through carefully memorized narratives.

As always, the poor tenant farmers suffered the most. Their lives were spent in labor, though they, too, sent their sons and daughters to the "hedge schools"; they, too, heard the bards, or *seanachies*, recite Irish history. A sorrowful history it was, Nano learned early on: a weave of invasions, battles, and repression. Her lay teachers had to stay one step ahead of the British constables. The priests traveled in disguise, and their people quietly hid them wherever they could: in barns, in sheds, and in concealed hearth-side hollows called "priest holes." The Nagles may have hidden priests themselves; such events were certainly never recorded.

In 1714, Honora "Nano" Nagle was born in Ballygriffin, Cork, the largest county in Ireland, spreading lush and green across its southwest corner. Garrett Nagle, her father, was descended from

Norman gentry; his wealthy family had more choices than many others of his faith. Nano was shielded from some of the injustices the poor had to bear. Many well-off Irish Catholics were educated on the continent, and the Nagles sent their older children to continue their studies in Paris.

Nano and her sister, Ann, had spent ten comfortable years in the glittering city of Louis XV. In Paris it was easier to forget the injustices at home—and in Paris, the Nagle girls enjoyed a vibrant social whirl. The French king's capital city was one of merriment, tolerance, and festivity.

It preserved a welcome atmosphere for the two young Irish women. Their father sent them ample funds so they could enjoy the "City of Light." Later, an old friend reminisced about this phase of Nano's life: "You have heard *sans doute* that she had been fond of the world when young, enjoyed its amusements, and when obliged to return from France to Ireland regretting its various enjoyments, she felt as if deprived of everything pleasant or desirable; yet I do not believe that she neglected the Main Point." Nano Nagle enjoyed her social entertainments until her conscience was stirred by an incident she never forgot. It cast a new and unflattering light on her "aimless life of pleasure."

Early one morning, Nano was returning home from a ball. Something across the street had caught her eye. There she noticed a group of poor people gathered in front of a church. The church doors were still locked, but the people waited patiently in the street and on the steps. Nano was struck by these devout people wishing to start their day with worship while she had been dancing the night away. This was no instant conversion experience—but the sight made an indelible impression upon her.

Garrett Nagle died in 1746 and, grieving for their father, the Nagle sisters returned from Paris to join their widowed mother in

Dublin. There, Nano Nagle became more aware of the poor. Mother Clare Callaghan has left us this account of Nano's watershed moment: "When living with her mother and sister in Dublin...[Nano] requested from her pious sister to get made up in a splendid silk dress, the materials for which she had purchased in Paris. She often said she was never so edified as when her sister disclosed to her in confidence that she had disposed of [sold] the silk for the purpose of relieving a distressed family. This circumstance, together with the death of this sister soon after, wrought so powerfully on the heart of Miss Nagle as perfectly to disengage it from the fashionable world from which she had tasted so much of, and enjoyed till then.

"She often said to her sisters in religion that it was this trifling circumstance which fired her determination to devote the remainder of her life to God in the service of the poor." This was the moment when everything changed for Nagle. This was the moment when a powerful inner decision was made. It was a definitive, costly choice.

On some level, Nano Nagle's mind and emotions must have been prepared for this radical turnabout. Unsure of what to do next, Nano went to visit her brother, David, at the family's home in Ballygriffin. There, she was further disturbed by watching the deteriorating life of the poor. Without enough inspiration, education, and guidance, the people were lapsing into ignorance, Nano feared. Their powerful faith seemed to her to be fading into superstition. Idleness and drunkenness was on the rise.

Education seemed to be the answer—but what could Nano do? She lacked the resources to change what she saw. Perhaps she wondered if one person could make a difference in so daunting a situation. Overwhelmed, she drew back and decided to enter a contemplative convent in France.

As a postulant, Nano must have sensed that God was calling her—but this enclosed convent did not seem to be the right place for her response to that call. After an intense inner struggle, Nano was encouraged by her spiritual director to return to Ireland. There she could minister to the children of the poor who haunted her mind and stirred her conscience. Return she did—immediately.

Nano's mother had died in her absence, and her brothers were living near the family's ancestral home in Ballygriffin. One of these brothers, Joseph, invited Nano to live with him and his wife in Cove Lane, south of Cork City. It was there she had time to think, to pray, to reflect. It was after this brief period that Nano Nagle began her life's mission: she would bring education to poor children—illegally. Her conscience prompted her to dare, to try.

One may wonder what turned the social butterfly into the "Lady With the Lantern." Certainly, the change in Nano Nagle's life was a daring move. She went from her privileged and protected class to become an illegal promoter of "subversive activity." Further, she made a drastic switch from wealth to poverty. Like Saint Francis and Saint Clare, she found this transition a joyous one. She was not the first to find emptiness in a life purely devoted to self-interest and pleasure. Again, Francis and many others had made the same discovery.

In 1754, Nano rented a mud hut just west of a chapel in Cove Lane. The hut had two rooms, an earthen floor, a garret and a thatched roof. To the modern eye, the place might have appeared quaint. To Nano's contemporaries, this makeshift "schoolhouse" would have been overlooked as a windowless hovel. That was exactly what would safeguard it from the authorities. To protect her own family, Nano did not even tell her brother or her sister-in-law about her project.

It is hard for us to appreciate how dangerous Nano's work was. The idea of teaching children their catechism seems harmless enough now. In 1749, however, it was considered a powerful way to raise up educated students who could restore Irish pride and perhaps, one day, a nationalist movement. Anyone who did this was a traitor to the king of England—and treason was a hanging offense. Nano's work would defy the British authorities—and ignorance itself.

Lantern in hand, Nano Nagle slipped through the countryside of Cork by night. Ducking through cottage doorways, she crouched by hearths and explained her purpose. Moving quietly down Willow Lane, Maypole Road, Donovan's Lane and Pender's Alley, she collected her pupils. At last, Nano Nagle received thirty girls in her mud-walled schoolhouse. She gathered them together in prayer and called her "classroom" to order for the first time. The entire enterprise was strictly illegal.

It did not take long for Joseph Nagle to hear about his sister's dangerous venture. He railed at her about the possibility of dire legal retribution, but to no avail. Nano remained true to her conscience—and eventually her brother gave his support to her growing mission.

So many parents wanted their children to attend Nano's school, she had to secure another cabin to accommodate them. In only nine months, two hundred children filled the two buildings and more were to come.

Praise for Nano's enterprise reached the parish of Saint Finbarr in northern Cork City. Its lanes and byways were peopled by poor workers in the meatpacking industry. They, too, saw the great need for education and approached Nano Nagle with a proposal: to open schools in their area, in return for financial compensation. Soon, Miss Nagle was providing classes to two hundred children on Philpot Lane near North Gate bridge.

Unfortunately, the north parishes did not contribute the promised funds, so Nano dipped into her own savings; she could not turn the growing numbers of children away. Providentially, her uncle Joseph Nagle died in 1757 and left his niece with considerable resources for continuing her mission. This she did, with an enduring sense of gratitude. Nano's school's curriculum included reading, spelling, and arithmetic, with the addition of needlework for the girls. Lay teachers were hired for these secular subjects, but the greatest emphasis was placed upon religious instruction, which Nano taught herself. All sessions started and closed with prayer. By 1769, Nano Nagle was running seven primary educational institutions, two of which were for boys.

As the schools grew and stabilized, Nano found herself increasingly drawn to private devotions. She also began to engage in other services to the poor, walking the lanes at night to visit the ill and indigent. Her signature lantern was always in her hand. One historian wrote that "there was not a single garret in Cork that she did not visit and did not know." Nano made these visits after teaching all day. Her evenings were spent alone, in prayer.

Once again, Nano's resources ran low. She took to begging for alms on the streets, where she was often taunted and jeered as "the old beggar." Unfazed, she dared to take her place with the poor on the streets. Gradually, her financial resources improved but at the same time, her health began to fail. Nano became deeply concerned about the future of her work and began to think of ways to safeguard it.

She had set up a solid network of schools, however illegal, and now she must protect it for posterity. In 1771, Nano persuaded French Ursuline nuns to help her, but this experiment failed. As an enclosed Order, the Ursulines could not go out to the homes of the poor.

One more act of daring was needed—and soon. Nano Nagle now knew she had advanced tuberculosis. After deep reflection, inspiration came: Nano would found her own order to run her schools and care for the indigent ill. This new congregation was founded on Christmas Day, 1775. Its small and humble beginnings did not indicate its future success. Only four women took their vows that Christmas Day—Nano was the first. She could not be given a religious habit, however; nor could her sisters.

Due to the penal laws, her little congregation had to remain "under cover," as did her schools. Nano Nagle continued with her work as long as her physical condition permitted. "If I could be of service in saving souls in any part of the world," she wrote, "I would gladly do all in my power."

Nine years after the founding of this secret Order, Nano knew she was dying. She asked to be buried in the public cemetery of Saint John near Cove Lane. Even in death, Nano wished to be in solidarity with the poor. On April 26, 1784, Nano Nagle received the Last Rites and blessed the small community that gathered around her bed. Her last words were, "Love one another...and spend yourself for the poor."

In 1805, Pope Pius VII gave official approval to her Presentation Order of Our Lady, which remains active today on every continent. Nano Nagle was a quiet rebel defying the highly punitive law of the land in oppressed Ireland. It is hard for us to imagine how repressive the British Penal Codes were for Irish Catholics—and how swift and harsh their enforcement. In some ways, Nagle seems to have some similarities with the American heroine Harriet Tubman, stealthily and steadily breaking unjust human laws for the sake of a higher law.

In other ways, Nagle's life is reminiscent of Elizabeth Seton's. Both women were raised in comfort, even luxury, and made the tough choice to surrender it all to serve God and neighbor at high personal risk.

Honora "Nano" Nagle is not a canonized saint, but it seems unlikely that this would have mattered to her. After her drastic change of direction, her life consistently brought light to others—and today, her lantern is the symbol of the religious Order she founded.

....

Questions for Reflection and Discussion

1. How would you define Nano Nagle's example?
2. What sustained her more than anything?
3. Was she motivated by faith or patriotism?
   Could she have been motivated by both?
4. What caused her life's turnaround?
5. Was Nano Nagle's "mission" nationalistic or spiritual?
6. Do you think she was "driven" or "called?"
   Could she have been both?
7. What can Nano Nagle's life teach us today?
8. Where do we need Nano Nagle's kind of commitment now?
9. Would you have changed your life as Nano did?
10. Where is "the moment of truth" for this heroine?

Sojourner Truth of Battle Creek (1797-1883)

Leave now, her friends advised. The place was bad. Talk was strong. Men were riled. They swore to attack any black preacher who spoke at this outdoor meeting. What, then, would they do to a black woman preacher? Consider, her friends warned: Leave now. She listened politely—and she listened to her inner voice. Surely God would shield her. She was his vowed servant. There was nothing to fear. She would stay.

Out she went, then, into the campgrounds—all six feet of her, long-striding, strong-built, a towering figure facing the crowd. Standing on a rise of ground, she sang a hymn in her big, deep voice. Suddenly, armed rioters surrounded her. Serene and sure, she scanned the crowd. She spoke; she sang again. "Her speech operated on the roused passions of the mob like oil on agitated waters," it was reported. She raised her voice in song one last time. Before she had finished, the mob was running away from her.

Who was she? Whose formidable presence could quell a riot? What force surrounded her with such uncanny calm? It was God's power, the speaker would have said. For God's sake, she had defied expectations, broken rules, risked her life, and forfeited safety to become a modern-day prophet.

Born a slave in Hurley, New York, in 1797, she was named "Isabella." Her mother had told "Belle" about God: "When you are beaten or cruelly treated, or you fall into any kind of trouble, you must ask for his help. He will always hear you and help you." Belle held to this as she passed from master to master. Married off to an older slave, she bore five children in six years—and longed for freedom. Mr. Dumont, her last master, promised to set her free in 1826.

When he went back on his promise, Belle held in her anger. She watched; she waited. She would defy her master yet. One night, she took her baby and, running through the dark, escaped through the woods. She knew her husband would tend to their other children. Belle's conscience told her that slavery was wrong; she must go free. Sheltered by a Quaker couple, the Von Wageners, Belle could not enjoy her freedom. At the Feast of Pentecost, there was always a great celebration in the slave quarters of her old plantation. Missing her children, Belle asked the Von Wageners if they would take her to see them for Pentecost. As she returned from the feast day, she was startled by a vision: It came "with the suddenness of a flash of light, showing her in the twinkling of an eye...that there was no place that God was not." But there was a loving presence, a figure she seemed to know.

"I know you and I don't know you....You seem perfectly familiar; I feel that you not only love me, but that you always have loved me—yet I know you not—I cannot call you by name." With every fiber of her being, Belle longed to know the figure's name. And then it came to her. It was Jesus, "through whom love flowed like a fountain." With that love flowing through her, she cried, "Lord, Lord, I can even love the white folks!" She said later that she walked around in a different world now, as if in a dream. But she dared not tell anyone for a while.

In time, Belle went to a nearby campground meeting. After listening to the testimony of others there, she was startled to learn that others knew about "her Jesus." One after another, people stood up and witnessed. "Why, that man's found him, too," she said to herself. And another, and another. Finally Belle concluded, "They all know him [Jesus]! I was so happy!"

For several years thereafter, she felt that Jesus was calling her to another life but she did not know what it was. Attentive to God, Belle worked as a maid in various homes. Meanwhile, she watched; she waited on the Lord. In 1843, while scrubbing an employer's floor, God's call came to Belle quite clearly: She was to quit being a servant to men and become the Lord's servant instead. Again, she did not comprehend what form this service would take. Even so, she would defy her expected role, just as she had defied slavery and conventional motherhood. She could do no less; her conscience prompted her to follow God's calling.

For her new life, Belle asked God for a new name. Immediately it came: "Sojourner Truth." Now she understood. She was to be a wandering preacher of the truth. God was truth and she belonged to God.

Sojourner Truth's "watershed moment" had come. She had made tough choices before—defying her status as a slave was one of them. Putting her faith in Jesus Christ was another. But this was the toughest choice of all.

Sojourner left everything behind and entrusted her entire life's direction to God. Like Mary Harris Jones, she went forward with nothing and risked everything. As an African American woman, Sojourner knew, she would meet with challenges, hostility, and very real physical risks. Rape and lynching were always possibilities for this stranger. And yet, Sojourner Truth took that risk, never showing fear, because her faith was strong enough to carry this strong soul even further.

As Sojourner Truth followed her calling, she carried only a pillow case containing a quarter, a loaf of bread, and a chunk of cheese. Traveling along the East Coast, she stopped and spoke at camp meetings, where she was usually welcomed. This, then, was her life's vocation: to travel "up and down the land, showing the people their sins and being a sign unto them." From her deep memory, she drew out powerful scriptural texts. Sojourner always concluded with a hymn and always began with the statement, "Children, I talk to God and God talks to me."

So composed was she, so biblically sound, so eloquent, Sojourner Truth soon developed a reputation as a powerful orator. Leaders of the abolitionist movement invited her to their meetings to speak against slavery. The great figures of her day respected and knew her: Frederick Douglass, William Lloyd Garrison, Harriet Beecher Stowe, and many others. A writer named Olive Gilbert persuaded Sojourner to dictate the story of her life. *The Narrative of Sojourner Truth*, privately published by Garrison, appeared in 1850. It was one of the first autobiographical stories about a former slave's life.

Throughout the 1850s, Truth's own fame grew. She was in great demand as a speaker and gave hundreds of talks. These were always delivered for her special causes, and she believed that God was guiding her choices—and her words. Her passionate commitment lay with two matters of conscience: abolition and women's rights. She lent her considerable energies to the *Ohio Anti-Slavery Bugle*, edited by Marius Robinson. In addition to her primary concerns, she spoke out on prison reform (which she supported) and capital punishment (which she opposed). By 1861, Sojourner Truth was one of the best-known women in America—and the guest of President Abraham Lincoln.

Sojourner's most famous speech was delivered at a large meeting in support of women's rights. Always defiant, often passionate, she stood up to speak. Hecklers shouted at her, insisting that women were, by nature, inferior to men. She let her sunbonnet drop to her feet as she drew herself up to her full height. Her gaze, reportedly, could be piercing. She threw back her Quaker shawl and bared her muscular right arm. Her rich and powerful voice filled the church where her listeners gathered. Her response to those hecklers is still printed and quoted today:

"Look at me!" she began. "Look at my arm! I have plowed and planted and gathered into barns and no man could beat me—and ain't I a woman? I could work as much and eat as much as any man—and bear the lash as well. And ain't I a woman? I have borne children and seen them sold into slavery, and when I cried out with a mother's grief, none but Jesus heard me. And ain't I a woman?

"He talks about intellect [a former speaker]. What's intellect got to do with women's rights or black folks' rights? If my cup won't hold but a pint and yours holds a quart, wouldn't you be mean not to let me have my little half-measure full? That little man in black there....He says women can't have as much rights as a man because Christ wasn't a woman....Where did your Christ come from? Where did he come from? From God and a woman. No man had nothing to do with it!

"If the first woman God ever made was strong enough to turn the world upside down all alone, we women together ought to be able to turn it back and get it right side up again. And now that we are asking to do it, the men better let us. [Picking up her bonnet, moving from stinging power to studied politeness:] Obliged to you for hearing me."

Her humor leavened her intensity. After a pessimistic speech by Frederick Douglass at an anti-slavery meeting, Sojourner spoke out to lift the pall over the room. "Frederick?" she asked wryly. "Is God dead?"

On another long and tiring speaking tour, Sojourner stopped for a talk in Florence, Massachusetts. Taking her place at the podium, she surveyed her audience and probably kept a straight face as she announced, "Children, I have come here like the rest of you—to hear what I have to say."

She would never be silenced. She never showed fear. With Sojourner's commanding presence, she could silence a crowd with her steady gaze over her wire-rimmed spectacles. She was on a mission for God—her conscience and her faith kept her "on message": The rights of the oppressed.

Quoting the Gospels and the Hebrew prophets, she struck a chord with most of her listeners. Whether she inspired them, challenged them, or angered them, they remembered Sojourner Truth. By all accounts she was a natural communicator, and her influence continued to spread. An incident in 1858 did not detract from her reputation. At a large gathering for women's rights in Battle Creek,

Michigan, another heckler accused Sojourner of being a man in women's clothes. Her answer was simple. She opened her blouse and silently exposed her breasts.

Sojourner Truth did not seem to care if her words were popular or challenging. She dared to take on sacred subjects with all the power she possessed. Her speaking continued as the Civil War broke out. She advocated the enlistment of black soldiers and actively recruited men of color to fight for the Union.

There is some controversy about the authorship of the song, "The Valiant Soldiers," written for the First Michigan Colored Regiment. Some sources say that Sojourner wrote its lyrics to the music of "The Battle Hymn of the Republic." This claim has been disputed but there is no dispute about Truth's commitment to African American troops.

After the Emancipation Proclamation was molded into the Thirteenth Amendment to the United States Constitution, Truth labored tirelessly for the National Freedman's Relief Association in Washington, D.C. She was appalled by the poor conditions of former slaves who had set up squatters' camps in the nation's capital. Her tall figure was a constant sight amid the desperate and dispossessed.

While working on behalf of these African Americans, she met with President Abraham Lincoln in 1864. Sojourner felt moved to offer encouragement to the sad-looking man. At the start of the following year, Truth felt she was called to serve as a nurse at Washington's Freedman's Hospital. There is no doubt that she joined most Americans in mourning the death of President Lincoln, which occurred while she was still in the District of Columbia, not so very far from Ford's Theatre.

By 1868, Sojourner was on the road again, touring up and down the East Coast. God continued to guide her, she believed, in championing the cause of the oppressed. During the 1870s, she returned to Washington in an effort to obtain federal land grants for ex-slaves. This daring attempt involved a protracted effort on Truth's part. She managed to meet with President Ulysses S. Grant at the White House but after several years this particular cause had failed. Sojourner Truth dared to take on unpopular causes and stand behind them.

Sojourner had a natural kinship with the downtrodden, much as Mary "Mother" Jones did. Although their ethnic origins are far apart, they both arose from the suffering classes who needed a voice. How intriguing that here in America, one of those voices had a Dutch accent and the other, an Irish lilt.

Although there is no record of Sojourner Truth meeting her sister abolitionist, Harriet Tubman, both women appeared at rallies for their cause during the same decade and both were outspoken in their defiant stand against slavery.

Wise and venerable as she aged, Sojourner must have realized that she would not live to see the successful resolution of most of her favored causes. This did not deter her preaching in the least. "I'm not going to die...," she told a friend. "I'm going home like a shooting star."

Truth dared to go where God called her, for as long as she had strength in her limbs and breath in her lungs. Lacking the means to travel abroad, she never got to London to see William Wetmore Story's statue, "The Libyan Sybil," inspired by none other than Sojourner Truth. She died before artist Frank Courtner was commissioned to paint the meeting between Truth and Lincoln. In the end, such honors may not have mattered to Sojourner Truth.

She knew her calling came from God. A preacher without a church, she had the largest congregation in America. Once enslaved, she had a well-known voice for liberation. Once homeless, she had a home with such luminaries as Wendell Phillips, Lucretia Mott, William Lloyd Garrison, and Susan B. Anthony, as well as her own house in Battle Creek, Michigan. There, on November 26, 1883, she died after a brief illness and was buried at Oak Hill Cemetery. Her life had nearly spanned America's eventful nineteenth century—a century that Sojourner Truth helped to shape.

Questions for Reflection and Discussion

1. How would you define Sojourner Truth's example?
2. What sustained her more than anything?
3. Was she motivated by faith or anger?
   Could she have been motivated by both?
4. Why do you think she changed her mind?
5. Was Sojourner a "publicity hound" or heroine?
6. Do you think she was wrong to leave her children for freedom?
7. What sacrifices did Truth make for her life as a traveling preacher?
8. Do we need Sojourner's kind of commitment today?
9. Would you have stood up to hecklers or slipped away?
10. Where is "the moment of truth" for this heroine?

Maria Skobtsova of Latvia
(1891–1945)

At the notorious Ravensbrück concentration camp, Mother Maria Skobtsova found herself living out her own words: her commitment was "to quench the world's sorrow with my own self." On Easter eve 1945, she stepped into a line of people herded toward the gas chambers. Some see this as an act of self-offering; others believe Mother Maria took the place of a frantic companion. One fact is indisputable: Mother Maria died willingly at Ravensbrück only a few days before troops liberated the camp.

Fifty-four years earlier, Mother Maria Skobtsova was born Elisabeth Pilenko in Latvia, a Russian province. The Pilenkos were devout Orthodox Christians, and Elisabeth was brought up in a religious home. Her father, an aristocrat, died when his daughter was only fourteen. "Lisa" was at an impressionable and rebellious stage. She met this loss with a drastic but predictable reaction. She turned away from God and became an ardent atheist. Her father's death seemed unjust to her. "If there is no justice, there is no God," she decided. When her family moved to Saint Petersburg in 1906, "Lisa" Pilenko immersed herself in a new atmosphere: Her companions now were free-thinking radicals, intellectuals, and literary figures. Only eighteen, she married a Bolshevik and began to write poetry. Eventually she published a collection of her work titled *Scythian Shards*, but her brief marriage ended in 1913. Perhaps religious conflict contributed to the divorce; her husband became a Roman Catholic. In any case, Pilenko's life continued to be turbulent.

The times themselves were troubled and Eastern Europe was shaken by the Bolshevik Revolution. In 1918, Elisabeth Pilenko became deputy mayor of Anapa, a town in southern Russia. Although she was now a member of the revolutionary party, she was deeply affected by the suffering caused by the Russian Revolution. Her awareness of the people's poverty and dislocation increased and she began again to read the gospels. She dared to apply to the Theological Seminary in Saint Petersburg and was the first woman to be accepted there. However, she never had a chance to attend the seminary; her life was moving too fast.

Abruptly, anti-Communist forces invaded Anapa; when the mayor disappeared, Pilenko found herself in charge. She was arrested and tried for being a Bolshevik—but she recognized the judge as a friend. Once her teacher, Daniel Skobtsova made sure that Pilenko was swiftly acquitted. Their relationship warmed after the trial, and they married in 1918.

After a peaceful interval, Communist forces again gained power and the Skobtsova family left Russia. They lived in the nation of Georgia, then Yugoslavia, and finally, in 1923, their odyssey ended in Paris. By that time, "Lisa" was the mother of three children and a student of social work and theology. In the French capital, her situation seemed to stabilize.

Only three years later, however, her youngest child, Anastasia, fell ill with influenza and died. "Lisa" was devastated; and as she grieved, the family she had tried to form began to unravel. Her marriage disintegrated. One child was sent to boarding school; her son, Yuri, lived with his father. Elisabeth Pilenko Skobtsova paused to take stock. She saw herself at a crossroads and felt the need to change her life's direction.

So far, that life seemed to be a series of misadventures. After two failed marriages, the loss of her country and her child, Elisabeth saw "a new road" before her and "a new meaning to life." She discerned a calling from God, decided "to be a mother for all, for all who needed maternal care, assistance, or protection." Wholeheartedly, she responded to this call to her life's true vocation. Here, then, was her watershed moment, her tipping point—her irrevocable choice to give her life to God.

Her conscience was stirred when she relocated to the city's center. It was teeming with impoverished Russian émigrés whose old lives had been swept away. Madame Skobtsova began a ministry to them wherever they were: in slums, in hospitals, and prisons. At the same time, she knew she was experiencing a deep spiritual conversion.

Intensely affected by Christ's suffering humanity, Skobtsova's Christianity reasserted itself in full force. "He also died," she wrote of Jesus. "He sweated blood....They struck him in the face."

Gradually, she began to see the suffering Christ in each refugee she encountered. "Each person," she wrote, "is the very icon of God Incarnate in the world. This realization signaled a significant spiritual awakening for her. Maria saw "the need to accept this awesome revelation of God unconditionally, to venerate the image of God" in every human being. As she continued her social work, her sense of calling deepened.

When her bishop suggested that she enter a convent, she recast her concept of monasticism: "The more we go out into the world, the more we give ourselves to the world, the less we are of the world." By now Skobtsova knew she had a religious vocation. Clearly though, she did not want to be a cloistered nun. What she hoped for was an active form of monastic life, defined by "the complete absence of even the subtlest barrier which might separate the heart from the world and its wounds."

Her bishop agreed to this recasting of an Orthodox nun's traditional role. Her husband assented to an ecclesiastical divorce, similar to an annulment. In 1932, Elisabeth Pilenko Skobtsova made her final profession as a "monastic in the world."

The beloved Orthodox priest and spiritual writer, Metropolitan Anthony Bloom, saw Mother Maria soon after she was professed and clothed in her new habit. "She was a very unusual nun in her behavior and her manners," Father Bloom wrote. "I was simply staggered when I saw her for the first time in monastic clothes. I was walking along the Boulevard Montparnasse and I saw, in front of a café, on the pavement, there was a table, on the table was a glass of beer and behind the glass was sitting a Russian nun in full monastic robes. I looked at her and decided that I would never go near that woman. I was young then and held extreme views."

With this new life, she received a new name: Mother Maria. Her community didn't comprise other nuns; rather, it was a community of refugees from revolution. Her cloister took the form of a rented house, containing a shelter, a soup kitchen, and a chapel. She had little time for ascetic practices associated with monasticism. "At the last judgment," she wrote, "I shall not be asked whether I was successful in my ascetical exercises, nor how many bows and prostrations I made. Instead, I shall be asked, 'Did I feed the hungry, clothe the naked, visit the sick and the prisoners.'"

While Mother Maria developed her rented house into a place of service, she slept on a cot in the cellar. At all hours, there were knocks at the door upstairs. Her residence became home to refugees, to the indigent, to the lost and hungry. Word of this shelter traveled through the alleys of Paris, and the house was always full. Volunteers helped Mother Maria, possibly members of a Russian Orthodox parish which sent Father Dmitri Klepinin to be the community's chaplain and Father Sergei Bulgakov as Mother Maria's confessor. Soon this unusual home expanded even further.

The Orthodox Church was in need of renewal. Here, in Mother Maria's shelter, an original organization was formed: Orthodox Action. This movement was recasting the way the Church functioned in the world, calling for a more radical approach to living out the gospel. How to make this concept into a reality? Maria's guests wondered.

Orthodox Action stressed the mandates of Jesus to wash one another's feet; to "love one another as I have loved you;" to care of the poor in an active fashion. There were various opinions on the application of the gospel to daily life, but a single warm-hearted will to hasten the coming of "the Reign of God."

It would have been interesting to view a cross-section of Mother Maria's house during the 1930s. On one side was the shelter, overflowing with the Russian refugees. On the other side was a kind of parlor where Russian émigrés exchanged ideas about applied theology. It is likely that the smell of hot borscht, or beet-stew, permeated both sides of this lively community. There was really no dichotomy between parlor and shelter. They formed two halves of one whole fruit.

Shuttling between kitchen and sitting rooms, Mother Maria seemed to be everywhere at once, enacting the very words she spoke. The 1930s may have been the happiest and most productive years of this new nun's life. At last she had found where God was calling her. At last she was living what she believed and following her conscience. And at last, she was mother to many. A woman of great empathy, Mother Maria seemed adept at identifying with the suffering—and yet, her emotional involvement did not drain or paralyze her.

She said her evening prayers in the chapel. Her night prayers were offered in the cellar, beside the furnace and her cot. Over her head, she knew her guests were sleeping—or talking late into the night about the Sermon on the Mount. Those were rich years for the Orthodox community in Paris, and for Mother Maria, but soon her life was sliding toward another crisis yet again.

With Hitler's rise to power just across the border, France sensed great danger drawing near. In 1939, the Nazis invaded Poland and precipitated world war. Then, in 1940, the fears of the French were realized. After valiant fighting, Paris was occupied by the German Army and controlled by Hitler's Third Reich. Mother Maria continued to act on her belief that every human being was an icon of God. Only now, this conviction carried grave consequences. Once more, Mother Maria's conscience was stirred. She and her chaplain, Father Dmitri, knew they were called to work with the French resistance. This, of course, meant taking a great risk: rescuing Jews.

Mother Maria had made radical changes before. She had redirected her life in major ways and finally, with her monastic vows, she had found her authentic calling. But she had never risen to this new challenge, this new risk, this toughest of all decisions. Since her commitment to venerate the image of God in every human being, how could she turn aside now? And yet, she must have known that she was putting her own life at risk—and perhaps those of her children and friends. This difficult decision was made quietly, with commitment and submission. She would remain true to her beliefs, even if it put her directly in harm's way.

Mother Maria may have wondered if she were jeopardizing her community's safety—but not for long. She could see no alternative to helping a persecuted people find safety. The project began with shelter. Soon, Jewish people came to her door, asking if Father Dmitri could make baptismal certificates for them. He could; he did. Still, this was far from enough. Working with the resistance, Mother Maria and Father Dmitri found ways to smuggle Jewish families and individuals out of Paris. Some were sent to England or Scandinavia. Others were hidden in the garrets and cellars of resistance workers and their contacts. Once again, the word passed through Paris. There was help from Mother Maria Skobtsova.

As the situation worsened, she wrote, "...be fearless in the face of the most daunting task, to generate the spirit of discipline, self-limitation, sacrifice and love, to lay down our lives for our friends, and to follow in Christ's footsteps to the Golgotha appointed for us."

By 1942, many Jewish Parisians were arrested and herded into a sports stadium not far from Mother Maria's house of hospitality. In her habit, she managed to get into the stadium where she ministered to its frightened prisoners for three days. She even managed to smuggle out some of the detained children. These she took home to her house, already overflowing. If anyone came looking for Jews, she said, she would show them an icon of Mary, the mother of Jesus.

In February 1943, the Nazis banged on the door of Mother Maria's house. She was arrested along with Father Dmitri, her son,

Ravensbrück concentration camp

Yuri, and an assistant in her work. When Father Dmitri was inter-rogated, a Gestapo officer demanded to know if the priest would stop his subversive activities.

"I can do no such thing. I am a Christian," Father Dmitri replied, "and must act as I must." After the Gestapo officer slapped him across the face, there were further questions. Father Dmitri held up his crucifix. "Do you know this Jew?" He challenged the Gestapo—and was knocked to the floor. With Mother Maria, her son, Yuri, and others, Father Dmitri was sent to the concentration camps. They were divided by gender: The men went to Buchenwald, the women to Ravensbrück. Somehow Yuri was able to smuggle out a note: "I am absolutely calm, even somewhat proud to share Mama's fate," he wrote. "Whatever happens, sooner or later we shall all be together. I can say in all honesty that I am not afraid of anything any longer....I ask anyone whom I have hurt in any way to forgive me. Christ be with you!" Mother Maria ministered to everyone she met at Ravensbrück.

Many survivors of that camp remembered her, and one of them wrote: "She exercised an enormous influence on us all. No matter what our nationality, age, political convictions—this had no significance whatsoever. Mother Maria was adored by all. The younger prisoners gained particularly from her concern. She took us all under her wing. We were cut off from our families, and somehow she provided us with family." This had been Mother Maria's strongest calling—to see God in everyone and to be a mother to all. She had more than lived out her vocation by the time she gave her life for another's and went to the gas chambers. "I am your message, Lord," she had written. "Throw me like a blazing torch into the night, that all may see and understand what it means to be a disciple."

On January 16, 2004, the Ecumenical Patriarch of Constantinople granted an official decree: the glorification (or canonization) of Mother Maria Skobtsova. She is a beloved saint in the Russian Orthodox Church.

....

Questions for Reflection and Discussion

1.   What did Maria Skobtsova's life teach you?
2.   What sustained her more than anything?
3.   What do you make of the huge change in her life?
4.   Do you think her early life detracts from her life as a nun?
5.   Was Maria's "mission" egocentric or heroic?
6.   Do you think she was lonely or "called?"
7.   What does Maria's life teach us now?
8.   Do we need Maria's kind of "conversion" today?
9.   Would you have risked your life for a persecuted minority?
10.   Where is "the moment of truth" for this heroine?

Satoko Kitahara of Tokyo (1929-1958)

Was she mad? People stared at her in the streets. What was a well-bred young woman doing with a ragpicker's wicker basket? Satoko only smiled. Sane, devout, and dedicated, she felt called by God to work in solidarity with the poor. This calling, however, defied every expectation of her family and her class. A daughter of privilege, she had led a comfortable life in the wealthy Tokyo suburb of Suginami.

Satoko's father, a professor, was descended from a long line of Shinto priests. Her mother had also grown up in a prosperous home. The Kitahara family owned a fine house and a garden so exquisite it was called "The Flower Manor." Satoko was destined for a traditional path: an arranged marriage and life as a deferential wife who must not offer opinions or challenge her husband. One day, she too would have a beautiful house, garden, and children.

But everything changed for Satoko with the advent of World War II. She and her brother joined other teens who worked at the Nakajima aircraft factory while bombs exploded overhead. Satoko survived; her brother did not. After the war's end, Americans flooded Tokyo and the young Japanese were taken with Western ways. Like any other privileged seventeen-year-old, Satoko was briefly attracted to the new styles in dancing, dressing, and entertainment. She later called this a "silly" time in her life.

Perhaps Satoko was seeking distraction from the harsh realities of post-war Japan. Hers was now a defeated nation, scarred by unprecedented bombing. Thousands were left homeless and displaced.

Satoko found that comfort and distraction were not enough to give her life meaning. Enrolled in a Catholic school, she felt attracted to the Mercedarian nuns who were her teachers. Satoko noticed that these sisters, interned during the war, were not bitter or resentful. In fact, they seemed to care for their Japanese charges. Satoko was impressed with Christ's call to love one's enemies, and soon she knew she was called to the Christian faith.

After her baptism in 1949, Satoko's existence took on a new meaning. The Mercedarians explained that those who followed Christ might suffer or even die as they "took up their cross" and followed their master. Even so, Satoko knew, there would be a purpose to such a life.

Her convictions grew stronger after she met Brother Zeno Zebrowski, a Franciscan friar who begged for the poor, then distributed his alms among them. Satoko recognized him as a holy man, an impression which was reinforced when she saw his photo in a newspaper. He was praying in one of Tokyo's most notorious slums, disparaged with the name "Ant Town." To the city council and to many of Tokyo's affluent, this community was a scandal. A squatters' settlement of ragpickers and junk dealers, it resembled an ant heap. It swarmed with hundreds of displaced persons, some of them drifters and former drug dealers.

However, the residents of Ant Town were proud. They kept strict rules for their community. Here there would be no crime—and no acceptance of charity. These, the working poor, watched out for each other by night and, by day, they collected junk from alleys and refuse bins. The scrap and rags were then sold at market, and so the people of Ant Town managed to survive.

Brother Zeno introduced Satoko Kitahara to this community—its orphans, its tin shelters, its campfires. That day made an indelible impression on the young woman from "the Flower Manor." Heeding Christ's call to serve the poor, Satoko felt she was called to do so. At Brother Zeno's request, she orchestrated a Christmas event at Ant Town. There she taught carols to the children and even set up a living Nativity scene. Food and drink accompanied the presentation. The media picked this up and put it on television, finishing the show with a rendition of *"Gloria in Excelsis Deo."* This event made for good press, but it didn't impress the leaders of Ant Town.

The community had its own hierarchy, and the two men in charge were suspicious of Satoko's presence. "The Boss," a reformed felon, and Matsui, called "The Professor," did not want the charity of some suburban "Lady Bountiful." A tasteful Christmas pageant would not solve any enduring problems there. Nor could a weekly suburban visitor understand how it felt to be poor and scorned. Moreover, Matsui was hostile to Christians and what he considered their hypocrisy. He was quick to communicate his feelings to Satoko.

"Thousands of years of what your religion calls charity have made no difference to the poverty of the world," he told her. "Yes, rich young ladies like you and nuns in fine robes get bored and take a stroll through the slums, scattering a few leftovers. That's the extent of Christian charity!" He made his criticism personal. "You in your fine two-story house, you wouldn't have a clue about the misery of people who live in destitution three hundred sixty-five days a year!"

Instead of feeling insulted, Satoko took his words seriously. They sounded like a confrontation from the prophets—and from Jesus himself. That confrontation marks Satoko Kitahara's most pivotal moment, one to which she had been building.

But after her response to that question, everything changed. The privileged daughter makes the decision of a lifetime: To live as one of the underprivileged—all for the sake of the Gospel.

Once again, we see a choice between service to self and service to others. Many other "defiant daughters" made a similar choice to serve a neighbor, no matter what guise that neighbor might take. Defying the perks and pleasures of wealth, Satoko Kitahara answered confrontation with a radically enacted commitment to her faith.

Matsui had left Satoko with a challenge—to read a Scripture passage from 2 Corinthians 8:9. As soon as she returned home, she found the verse and felt it go directly to her bones: "For you know the gracious act of our Lord Jesus Christ, that for your sake he became poor although he was rich, so that by his poverty you might become rich."

Satoko had reached her watershed moment; she felt that those words were meant for her. "I had thought I was a great Christian because I condescended to dole out some free time," Satoko said later.

"There was only one way to help those ragpicker children: become a ragpicker like them." And so, Satoko came to push her wicker basket through the back alleys of Tokyo, begging and scrounging for scrap to recycle. By the end of her first day, she had filled her basket and gathered enough discarded hemp to net a hundred yen at market. "The Boss" and "The Professor" were impressed. Her mother was horrified and quickly threw Satoko's clothes into boiling water. The next day, however, her daughter was back on the streets. "The Professor" had honored Satoko with her own junk cart. In the late afternoons, Satoko extended her ministry, setting up a rudimentary school for the children. There she tried to make education appealing, mixing grammar lessons with singing and dancing.

Eventually, Satoko rented a flat in Asakusa, near Ant Town. She exchanged her expensive garments for cheap serge trousers, a shirt, and a cap. Every day began with Mass and in time, some of the children accompanied her. After her stint at collecting junk, Satoko expanded the activities of the school she had created. Bath time followed. With her rosary at her waist, Satoko was observed with soap and towels in hand, giving Ant Town's children a thorough washing. Her image and her story appealed to the media, and once again she was photographed and interviewed. Dubbed "The Mary of Ant Town," Satoko saw the publicity as an advantage for her community.

Although her health was failing, Satoko continued with her work. Photographs of her with her junk cart appeared in national newspapers. She began to be viewed as a kind of folk heroine; a holy woman of the people. Numerous letters went out to her from all over Japan. Her prayers were requested and her own letters were treasured. Satoko was not interested in her continuing publicity but in her mission. Her years at Ant Town seem to have been the happiest of her life. "I do not intend to work just for my own eternal salvation, closing my eyes to the people around me....If my sufferings can help achieve that, what a joy," she said.

Satoko had always been delicate, subject to sporadic bouts with tuberculosis. Ant Town dampness and her own exertions finally overcame her weak constitution. Her health collapsed and, depressed, she had to return to her family's home in Suginami. Satoko was distressed. "I want to share the life of the Ant people. I want to work and suffer with them, to rejoice with them as one of them," she said. Before she could even consider that, however, Satoko was forced to take a cure in the mountain air for several months.

When she finally came back to Ant Town, Satoko was jolted by an emotional shock. Two new people were continuing the work she had begun: teaching and tending the community's children. Satoko was devastated and confused. She began to consider a sense of calling to become a Mercedarian nun; Mother Angela welcomed the idea.

Another piece of news heartened Satoko. Because of her example, "The Professor," Matsui, and the other leaders of Ant Town decided to be baptized. Even so, Satoko would not be satisfied until she could return to Ant Town and live there among the people who were now her family; her community.

That community was now in serious danger. The city authorities had wanted to be rid of the shantytown for years. To them, it was a blot on their city's image. They felt that Ant Town's land would serve Tokyo better as a public park. Satoko was stricken at the news. If the ruling council went through with the eviction, she vowed that she would go on a hunger strike before city hall, fasting and praying until Ant Town was saved—or Satoko died. Her national fame made this vow a serious challenge to the municipal government. It is also said that one of Tokyo's officials was moved by her promise. It is difficult to determine which influence was greater.

While this drama was unfolding, Satoko became feverish. As her temperature climbed, her doctor declared her to be in critical condition. He doubted that she would recover this time, but he offered an unexpected suggestion. He persuaded the Kitahara family to return Satoko to Ant Town. "She will probably die here," he observed. "But if she dies at Ant Town, she will die happy." When this news reached "The Professor," he and "The Boss" arranged special quarters for Satoko in her chosen community. There, her favorite holy objects were set out all around her.

Friends visited her and, with her growing happiness, Satoko's health began to improve a bit. Satoko was there, in her adopted home, when the city council decided to sell a new tract of land to Ant Town. Previously, the council had wanted to disband the place altogether but now, due to Satoko's publicity—and prayers, it was said—the city fathers would simply offer to relocate Ant Town.

The proposal seemed sincere and "The Professor" left to attend a crucial meeting with Tokyo officials. From her bed, Satoko gave Matsui her treasured rosary to take with him into the meeting. She promised to pray for Ant Town throughout the negotiations.

"The Professor" came back to his community with good news. The city council had decided to relocate Ant Town to new lands for the price of fifteen million yen, due within the next five years. The ragpickers' leaders calculated that this sum could be managed within that time frame. The community agreed and, on January 20, 1958, Ant Town was resettled on its new site. Satoko Kitahara was too ill to move with her friends, but her extended family always credited her prayers with its salvation. She had hung onto life until she knew Ant Town was safe.

Three days after the community moved and seven years after she joined it, Satoko Kitahara died in Tokyo. She was buried in Tama Cemetery, and her grave still draws pilgrims. In 1975, The Order of

Franciscan Conventuals became the promoters of Satoko's cause for beatification. Archbishop Shirayanagi of Tokyo furthered her cause in 1984. Satoko Kitahara's brief life became known worldwide. Her biography has appeared in several anthologies, and her biography, *The Smile of a Ragpicker*, by Paul Glynn, was published by the Marist Fathers in 1992. Satoko leaves us her own words in her own book, written in 1953, *The Children of Ant Town*. The story of Satoko Kitahara resonates with many. Knowingly or not, she was influenced by the "Little Way" of Saint Therese of Lisieux.

Another holy woman who died young of consumption, Therese advocated doing small, everyday things with the love of Christ. Satoko's life is also congruent with Mother Teresa of Calcutta, who was herself influenced by Saint Therese. Satoko Kitahara challenges the way we look at the poor. Her life is both inspirational and confrontational to all who work with the homeless and destitute in the name of Jesus.

Questions for Reflection and Discussion

1. How would you sum up Satoko Kitahara's example?
2. What sustained her more than anything?
3. Was she motivated by faith—or rebellion?
4. What got Satoko through her work at Ant Town?
5. Was Satoko's "mission" eccentric or heroic?
6. Do you think she was wrong to renounce her parents?
7. Do you sense the depth of Satoko's calling?
8. Where do we need Satoko's courage today?
9. Would you move to Ant Town?
10. Where is "the moment of truth" for this heroine?

Fannie Lou Hamer of Ruleville (1917–1977)

The granddaughter of a slave, Fannie Lou Hamer grew up chopping cotton twelve hours a day in Ruleville, Mississippi. Hers was a family of sharecroppers: hardworking, poorly housed, and scantily clothed. Despite their circumstances, Fannie Lou's strong mother instilled in her child two vital qualities: self-esteem and religious devotion.

"I want you to respect yourself as a black child, and as you get older, you respect yourself as a black woman," Lou Ella Townsend instructed Fannie Lou. "If you respect yourself enough, others will have to respect you."

This lesson was well-remembered, along with the example of living out the Gospel every day, no matter what happened. Both of Fannie Lou's parents were devoted Baptists. Her father was a "deeply religious man," and her mother, after a long working day in the fields, would always kneel down in prayer.

Drawing on Christian teaching, they counseled Fannie Lou against hatred. "Ain't no such of a thing as I can hate and hope to see God's face," Hamer wrote. "Christianity is being concerned with your fellow man." She was able to balance this belief with a strong sense of justice. "Christ was a revolutionary person, out there where it was happening" she stated. "That's what God is all about, and that's where I get my strength."

Fannie Lou Hamer would need all her strength for the struggle that lay ahead of her. She had already begun thinking about improving life for her people. "Sometimes I be working in the fields and I get so tired I say to the people picking cotton with us, 'Hard as we have to work for nothing, there must be some way we can change this.'"

Even so, she had no idea how to implement her thoughts—until August 27, 1962, when Hamer attended a meeting at Williams Chapel Missionary Baptist Church. There, a rally was sponsored by the Southern Christian Leadership Conference (SCLC) and the Student Nonviolent Coordinating Committee, (SNCC). Both organizations would change Hamer's path forever. At forty-five, with her husband's support, Hamer began a new life at that meeting. Its sponsors reminded the audience of its constitutional right to vote—and vote out politicians who were oppressing African Americans.

This was a revolutionary statement in the segregated Mississippi Delta of that era. A minister with SNCC, the Reverend James Bevel, preached a powerful sermon, "Discerning the Signs of the Time." He took as his text Luke 12:52, which focuses on this subject.

Bevel urged his listeners to recognize the signs of their own times, like clouds in the sky presaging rain. The rally stirred Hamer's soul; she had reached "the tipping point" of her life. At the church, she signed up to register at the courthouse and encouraged seventeen others to go with her. It seems almost incredible to us now, but Hamer, as an African American in Mississippi's Delta, had never been told she had the right to vote.

Fannie Lou was embarking on a dangerous mission. "I guess if I'd had any sense I'd a been a little scared," she commented later, but she added: "The only thing they could do was kill me and it seemed like they'd been trying to do that a little bit at a time since I could remember."

The fervor of the movement gained momentum. On the appointed day, Hamer's group rode to the Indianola courthouse and attempted to register to vote. Personal information was taken and a literacy test was administered. This was often used as a calculated stumbling block, and Hamer failed the test. Privately, she vowed to come back and take the test again—as often as she had to in order to pass.

As they returned to Ruleville, Hamer's group was stopped by local police officers in Indianola. The eighteen passengers were commanded to get off the bus; the driver seemed headed for jail. Inspired by the spirit of the Civil Rights Movement, Fannie and her comrades started to accompany him, singing the hymn, "Have a Little Talk With Jesus." The officers, fearing trouble, collected a $30 fine from the "Indianola Eighteen" and allowed them to get back on the bus and go home.

However, Hamer soon discovered that she might not have a home much longer. Here was her first test of conscience. Her employer and landlord gave her a choice: She must withdraw her voter registration—or leave her house and job. Hamer could not undermine others' opportunity to vote. Her stand for principle lined up with everything the Bible said about oppressing the poor. With her husband's support, she defied her boss. Refusing to withdraw her registration, she moved out of her family's home that night—and followed her conscience.

Fannie Lou Hamer stayed with a series of friends, but violence seemed to trail her wherever she went. The first incident occurred only ten days after her attempt at voter registration. Her hosts' house was attacked—sixteen bullets pierced their windows. No one was injured—but no one regarded this drive-by shooting as a coincidental happening.

Now living like hunted fugitives, Hamer and her husband left town. Again, Hamer faced a test of conscience. Was she giving in? Was she letting the oppressors win? After prayerful considerations, the Hamers returned to Ruleville, convinced that they should not act like frightened criminals. Defiant again, Hamer stepped up her civil rights activities. Undeterred by death threats, Hamer found her resolve strengthening.

In 1963, Fannie Lou Hamer was arrested with a group of protestors in Charleston, South Carolina, after deliberately entering a "whites-only" bus terminal. With her comrades, Hamer was thrown into jail, where she was brutally beaten. "It was the most horrifying moment of my life," she observed years later. Taunts and insults accompanied the blows, which had a lasting effect on her health. She was left with damaged kidneys, a stiffened body, and a blinded left eye. Even as she suffered from her injuries, she stayed strong in spirit. Some days afterward, she turned to one of the men who had beaten her and demanded, "Do you ever think or wonder how you will feel when the time comes you have to meet God?"

In jail for three days, Fannie Lou worked hard to keep up her comrades' spirits. Her courage is still remembered, and her encouragement often took the form of music. Hamer lifted up her voice so all could hear her singing, "This Little Light of Mine," and "When Paul and Silas Were Bound in Jail." Her group was also heartened by Hamer's extensive knowledge of Scripture and her ability to quote it from memory. Members of SNCC finally saw to the protestors' release, but the threat of violence haunted them all. It seems that the more opposition Hamer encountered, the more diligent she became.

Soon Hamer took action with the help of SNCC. They decided to join together and form a political party of their own: The Mississippi Freedom Democratic Party. She was now a fully engaged civil rights activist. In addition to campaigning for voter registration, Hamer was often called in to mediate and calm angry crowds with her eloquent speaking.

Her work extended to food and clothing drives for poor African Americans, a cause for which she was also harassed. She must have taken this as a sign that she was doing something right. She remained at a high level of involvement with her chosen causes.

"She was the quintessential itinerant activist," writes Chana Kai Lee, in her book *For Freedom's Sake.* "In her public appearances, Hamer displayed a folksy style that was effective; it enthralled. What she symbolized was just as important as the message and the cause, which was true for most of her movement career."

One of Hamer's proudest moments was a return from the road to Ruleville in 1964. The local newspaper reported: "Thirty-three Ruleville Negroes celebrated the return of local leader Mrs. Fannie Lou Hamer from a month-long speaking tour by going to the

Sunflower Courthouse to register July 21. All thirty-three were processed by the registrar."

One wonders about the personal cost of Hamer's work. It must have taken a tremendous physical toll on her, as well as on her personal life. However, she believed the Civil Rights Movement was fundamentally a spiritual one, sanctioned by Scripture's understanding of God's care for the oppressed. Perhaps she was able to make sacrifices because, as she said, Christ was her guide and Christ was "out where it was happening."

In one of her famous speeches, she quoted Ephesians 6:11–12, which says, "Put on the armor of God so that you may be able to stand firm against the tactics of the devil. For our struggle is not with flesh and blood but with the principalities, with the powers, with the world rulers of this present darkness, with the evil spirits in the heavens."

"This is what I think about when I think about my own work in the fight for freedom," declared Fannie Lou Hamer. In another speech, she offered one of her most famous sayings: "No one is free until everyone's free." Hamer rose to that self-imposed challenge in 1964.

On August 21, she led sixty-eight protestors to the Democratic National Convention. Their purpose was to challenge the seating credentials of the all-white Mississippi delegation. That hot summer in Atlantic City, New Jersey, Fannie Lou Hamer brought her cause to the entire nation's attention. Her Mississippi Freedom Democratic Party was under FBI wiretap surveillance, initiated by President Lyndon B. Johnson, who did not want any "incidents" to disrupt the convention—or any walkouts by Southern delegations. Once again, Fannie Lou Hamer remained true to her cause and her conscience. Her mission did not turn out precisely as she had hoped, but it impacted America in a different way.

Fannie Lou began this mission with a rally at the Union Baptist Church, which became her party's temporary headquarters. There, the MFDP organized their efforts, although they knew that their chance of success was small. Biographer Lee states that this challenge was more than a symbolic gesture, however. It would call the country's attention to the Civil Rights Movement at the peak of that movement's momentum.

At a key hearing, Fannie Lou Hamer gave testimony that was nationally televised. With her own style of eloquence, she was able to make the country aware of her cause as never before. By the time she finished recounting her experiences of brutality in jail, several on-site listeners were in tears.

Hundreds of sympathetic telegrams began arriving at MFDP headquarters. Arthur Waskow, a staunch supporter, observed in a written report on the convention, "Fannie Lou Hamer has agreed to be its star." For a time, her case seemed strong, and that evening, a television news program broadcast her entire testimony.

Hamer lobbied other delegations, attended meetings, and met with such important figures as Roy Wilkins, Martin Luther King Jr., and Joseph Rauh. Johnson and his supporters were said to be concerned by this continuous activity.

As the delegates moved closer to compromise with the MFDP's demands, Senator Hubert Humphrey began to waffle on this issue and distance himself from his traditional liberal position on civil rights. Fannie Lou Hamer took him on. "Senator Humphrey," she confronted him, "I been praying about you; and I been thinking about you, and you're a good man, and you know what's right. The trouble is you're afraid to do what you know is right. You just want this job [vice president]...but Humphrey, if you take this job, you won't be worth anything. Mr. Humphrey, I'm going to pray for you again."

In the end, after days of negotiation, Hamer's party not only failed to unseat the official Mississippi delegation, her group was evicted from the convention. Lyndon Johnson chose to protect the white Southern politicians. Even so, Hamer's party had drawn intense national interest in civil rights in America and made a lasting impression on its people, black and white.

As she left Atlantic City, Fannie Lou Hamer was not triumphant, she was angry. "We followed all the laws that the white people themselves made...," she said. "But we learned the hard way that even though we had all the laws and righteousness on our side, the white man is not going to give up his power to us....We have to take it for ourselves."

Chana Kai Lee aptly evaluates Hamer's efforts in 1964. "Whether the final outcome of the challenge was seen as a loss or a victory, the MFDP stand in Atlantic City was undoubtedly historically significant....The stand marked the beginnings of the [white] supremacists' demise, in the eyes of many." It also caused the shocking exposure of Mississippi's racial injustice; this exposure may have contributed to the 1965 Voting Rights Act. Finally, the events of 1964 made Fannie Lou Hamer a national leader in the ongoing cause of civil rights. One wonders how often she had to remind herself of her parents' prohibition of hatred.

In fact, Hamer did not let hatred stop her. Instead, she became deeply involved with anti-poverty work, including a strong stand for low-cost housing. In 1969, she founded what would become the Freedom Farm Corporation, designed to meet the economic needs of poor African Americans. Land was acquired for large-scale vegetable cultivation. The National Council of Negro Women donated fifty pigs, who quickly multiplied.

Three years later, Freedom Farm was distributing thousands of pigs to needy families. By 1972, the farm had built over seventy houses for people whose only homes had been shacks. Fannie Lou Hamer was involved with every aspect of this project, speaking all over the country to raise needed funds.

"I'm sick and tired of being sick and tired," Hamer famously remarked; this sentiment always drew laughter and agreement from her listeners. Until her final illness, however, she continued to work for the weary, the poor, the oppressed; she participated in Martin Luther King Jr.'s unfinished Poor People's Campaign. Hamer proved herself to be tireless on behalf of the tired.

One might wonder if Hamer had any regrets in her last years about her choice in mid-life: undertaking all-consuming causes that would outlive her. Certainly her personal life was altered, although her husband, Perry "Pap" Hamer was ever supportive of his wife. Still, they both decided to sacrifice time together for the sake of conscience and the call of a just God.

In Fannie Lou Hamer's transcribed autobiography, there is not a jot of regret. There are touches of righteous indignation and flashes of impatience. There is a constant devotion to God—and to God's oppressed people. And there is humor. Before her death from cancer in 1977, Hamer left instructions for the epitaph on her tombstone. On the stone, under her name, is her signature quotation: "I'm sick and tired of being sick and tired."

....

Questions for Reflection and Discussion

1. How would you define Fannie Lou Hamer's example?
2. What sustained her more than anything?
3. Was she motivated by faith or anger? Could she have been motivated by both?
4. Would you lose your home for a principle?
5. Was Fannie Lou Hamer's "mission" hate-filled or heroic?
6. Do you think she was "driven" or "called?" Could she have been both?
7. Does Fannie Lou Hamer's life inspire or intimidate you?
8. Do we need Fannie Lou Hamer's kind of commitment today?
9. Would you dedicate your life for others' rights, at all costs?
10. Where is "the moment of truth" for this heroine?

SECTION THREE

Daughters of Dedication

FOR ALL THE SAINTS WHO LIVE BEYOND US
WHO CHALLENGE US TO CHANGE
THE WORLD WITH THEM,
WE PRAISE YOU, O GOD.

Perpetua of Carthage
(181-203)

Perpetua (left) and Felicity of Carthage

The sight of two young women, stripped naked in the Carthage arena, drew uncharacteristic pity from the stadium's crowd. Perpetua, at twenty-two, and Felicity, her servant, seemed equally vulnerable. A small mercy was granted them: They were allowed to dress before they faced the wild beasts.

This gesture was highly unusual in a culture that reveled in such "sport." Gladiators faced lions, as did criminals—and under Roman law, Christians were traitors. Traitors were tortured and publicly executed; these events were commonplace. Even so, it was unusual for onlookers to shudder when they saw the human "combatants" enter the ring.

There was something about Perpetua that moved people deeply. Maybe it was her youth; maybe it was her motherhood. According to Saint Augustine, her *Passion Narrative* resounded through the churches of North Africa. Her story inspired other Christians who would become the next martyrs for the faith. Their courage and confidence bewildered their captors and confounds many of us today.

Some modern historians question the martyrs' motives. Did they have delusions of glory? Were they duped by an ecstatic sect? Or perhaps they showed a kind of faith-filled courage so rare that it baffles mere observers. In his book, *What Would You Die For?*, James J. Walsh probes that question. Walsh notes that early Christian martyrdom was seen in a religious context: it united the believer with the sufferings of Jesus on the cross.

Some Christian writers made the following point: "Whether we die is not the issue...we all die eventually...but how we die and the consequences of the manner of our death (are key)." This theme is repeated in later centuries as well.

By paying the ultimate price, a Christian also unites and inspires the faith of many others—though not all were able to live up to this calling. "Despite the benefits that many Christians saw in suffering martyrdom," Walsh observes, "many Christians failed when put to the test." Some could not face the torments of the arena, despite the excitement, devotion, and fervor of the new religion.

Perpetua was not one of these. In the arena, when a Roman tribune costumed her as the goddess Ceres, Perpetua had the temerity to protest: "We have come here of our own will precisely so as not to have our freedom crushed; we resigned our lives precisely so as not to have to do something like this. And we made this agreement with you."

The tribune gave in, allowing Perpetua and her companions to assume their original dress for their final hour. Perpetua's servant, Felicity, summed up their attitude. "What I suffer now, I suffer alone. But in the arena another will be with me...." A daughter of wealth and education, Perpetua was arrested with her comrades and charged with conversion to Christianity: a crime.

Repeatedly, she was asked to deny this, and those were the moments that divided and transformed her life. Despite the threats and pleas of her father, despite her love for her child, Perpetua could not bring herself to deny who she was. "*Christiana sum,*" she answered every question at her trial: "I am a Christian." This, of course, was the wrong answer if one wished to survive—and how easy it would have been to escape punishment. All Perpetua need do was renounce her faith, deny Christ, and offer incense to the Roman gods. But this was precisely what she could not do, no matter the cost.

In Robert Bolt's award-winning play, *A Man for All Seasons*, Sir Thomas More faces a similar dilemma. Although he is lord chancellor of England, More cannot go against his conscience or his faith. Like Perpetua, his stance lands More in prison. His beloved daughter begs her father to speak the words of a crucial oath—while thinking otherwise.

God, she says, will know More's heart. Again, like Perpetua, More cannot obey the pleas of his loved ones. It is interesting that his response is considered noble, while Perpetua's is dismissed as hysterical or deluded by some historians.

Perpetua withstood great pressure to rethink her stand. The intensity of this pressure appears throughout her journal, kept during her imprisonment prior to trial. Through her own words, we hear a calm and consistent voice—not the ravings of a fanatic. We hear her father's more emotional voice, alternating between taunts and pleas. We hear Perpetua's patient response to him, coupled with sorrow for his inability to know the comfort of her new-found faith.

Most touching is Perpetua's love for her young child, recently weaned. It consoled her, she wrote, that he was placed with a good family. Like Thomas More, Perpetua believed that her fidelity to her faith transcended all other bonds, even that of motherhood. This "defiant daughter's" stand may be the most difficult for us to understand. The zeal of the young Christian faith was different from anything we know today, and Perpetua was living in a radically different context. Perhaps Perpetua may have thought that her greatest gift to her child was her own adherence to principle. That would be her legacy to her son.

By contrast, how could she leave a legacy of lapsed faith in a time of danger? What sort of example would that set for a child; especially one raised in the new Christian community? Such thoughts may have gone through Perpetua's mind before she made her costly decision—and remained steady, serene, and resolute from that moment on.

Even so, we may wonder at this young woman's decision to leave her child for the sake of conscience. Renounce your faith or renounce your family: this was the agonizing choice. If we view Perpetua's decision in the context of her times, her choice becomes a bit clearer.

In the Roman Empire, Christian martyrs were often highly respected bishops and elders whose witness was important to the followers of Christ. Their example encouraged the young Christian community, a threatened minority even in sophisticated cities like

Carthage. Despite persecution, the new religion was in a state of high enthusiasm and deeply felt faith. A martyr paid the ultimate price, as did Jesus himself.

Christians were noticeable for their refusal to take part in pagan festivals. These lavish holidays provided people with their only recreation and pleasure—the Roman Empire did not allow weekend breaks from the daily routine. Unlike everyone else, Christians and Jews avoided the festivals because these were also religious occasions, held to thank the Roman gods. The empire's citizens resented Jews and Christians for their refusal to participate in citywide celebrations—and the Christians were the most vulnerable.

Unlike the Jewish community in Carthage, ancient and well-established, Christianity was new, unfamiliar, and suspected of secret barbaric practices. The sacrament of the Eucharist was misinterpreted as cannibalism. "There was no other cult quite like Christianity," writes Walsh. "From the Roman point of view, the Christians were a movement without a traditional identity defined by ancestral customs. They merited no tolerance." In fact, harassment and persecution of Christians was commonplace and condoned. Against such hostility, early Christians banded together more closely; for them, martyrdom demonstrated the self-giving love of the crucified Christ. Perpetua, a literate and cultivated woman, would have known this.

She might have lived a life of pleasure and comfort with her father, himself a pagan. Instead, she renounced such an existence—for belief; for faith; for Christ. By the time she became a Christian catechist, soon to be a convert, she belonged to a new community. Some historians assume that Perpetua's pagan husband abandoned her because of her faith, since he is never mentioned in her detailed *Passion Narrative*. Perpetua, then, was already familiar with sacrifice and suffering well before she entered the Carthage arena.

There were other avenues she might have taken. If the young Christian community sensed another wave of persecution coming, some members acted quickly. They fled. In fact, this might have been an attractive option. A refugee could save his or her life without renouncing the faith.

Even the great saint and church father, Polycarp, was warned to leave his city and so he did, quietly disappearing for a time. In the end, however, his conscience grew uneasy. He returned to his home and died under persecution about 150. Others were less courageous; they never returned to their Christian community and lapsed back into paganism instead.

A different way out was sheer bribery. Roman officials could—and did—overlook an arrest warrant for the right price. Such tactics were more common during later persecutions, particularly those that extended across the entire empire. The historian Tertullian notes with distaste that some Christian congregations practiced bribery *en masse*.

If this practice seemed too abhorrent, there was yet another option: to deny one's faith in public, only to return to its practice among friends. Community confession and penance might have seemed preferable to the fatal bite of a wild leopard. As Margaret More implored her father, such a statement was merely an external "formality." To the faithful, however, denying one's Christianity was no mere formality. It was a denial of God Incarnate, who said, "No greater love is this, that a man lay down his life for his friend."

They cited the agony of Jesus in the Garden of Gethsemane, where he sweated blood as he contemplated the crucifixion. Jesus prayed, "My Father, if it is possible, let this cup pass from me; yet, not as I will, but as you will." (Matthew 26:39). This became a part of the communal story and part of one's redemption.

Strength was also found in Jesus' Sermon on the Mount. Among the Eight Beatitudes is one that particularly consoled Christians under arrest: "Blessed are you when they insult you and persecute you and utter every kind of evil against you (falsely) because of me. Rejoice and be glad, for your reward will be great in heaven. Thus they persecuted the prophets who were before you." (Matthew 5:11–12). This turns our usual categories upside down, as do most of the Gospel values.

Perpetua, fluent in Greek, would have known this text and must have referred to it. Perhaps it tipped the scales for her. Perhaps loyalty to her new community was a factor in her decision: her new "family," in effect.

Some authors psychologize her decision as one made for glory, in which she claimed "her own personal autonomy." To others, however, the price for this fleeting status seems very high. Her death would be brutal, painful, and humiliating, and end forever her maternal role in her son's life. Perpetua's diary shows her keen awareness of this price.

After reflecting on Perpetua's own words, one may well affirm that her sustaining faith outweighed any other consideration. That faith was reinforced by her vivid dreams (also fodder for psychological hindsight) in prison. In one, Perpetua sees herself climbing a stairway to heaven. In another, she does battle with the devil—and wins. Her confidence is balanced by compassion for those she must leave behind. This balance mitigates against the "hysteria" theory of the "glory" hypothesis.

Perpetua's behavior speaks for itself in the course of her martyrdom, recorded by an eyewitness and friend. On the evening before her ordeal, she shared an "agape supper" with her fellow prisoners, a communal meal strongly associated with the Eucharist. At that point, she turned her journal over to a comrade-in-arms, who described the events of the following day—the day when she would defy death itself with her Christian faith.

The next morning, after a Christian man was sent to the arena—and survived—Perpetua and Felicity were called. As noted earlier, the crowd was moved by the sight of them and so they were dressed as they confronted the enemy: a wild heifer. The maddened cow charged Perpetua, who fell. Some historians describe another form of torture: The women were tied up in a net and dragged around the arena.

After the heifer tossed her, Perpetua noticed that her legs were exposed. She pulled her robe down over her thigh, protecting her modesty, even at that juncture. Then she asked for a pin so she could "fasten her hair, for it was not fitting for her to endure martyrdom with her hair in disarray, since she might seem to be mourning in her moment of glory...."

Other details reveal a bit more. When Perpetua saw her servant, Felicity, had been knocked to the ground, Perpetua helped her up and took her hand. Then the women stood together in the vast arena; two slight figures, holding hands like children, and the sight of them "conquered the cruelty of the crowd." There were no dividing lines between them now.

Perpetua sent for her brother and a comrade and told them: "Stand firm in your faith, love one another, and do not let our suffering weaken you."

With another prisoner, Perpetua and Felicity were brought to a part of the arena selected by the crowd. It was the area where survivors had their throats cut. Knowing this, the two young women exchanged a ritual kiss of peace. Then Perpetua laid her neck bare. The inexperienced executioner did not strike a clean blow. He cut Perpetua in the collarbone and she cried out in pain. According to an eyewitness, it was she who guided the soldier's sword to her own throat.

For many, the enduring image of Perpetua is this: A young woman resembling "a tender girl," reaching out her hand to her servant so they could face death together, as equals. With this gesture, Perpetua manifests the Christian message of brotherly and sisterly agape, despite the world's classes and distinctions. One imagines the two women holding hands, standing firm, as thousands of enemies looked on from their seats.

And what did they see? Two wasted lives? Two glorious heroines? Two drupes of a misbegotten sect, doomed to fail? "There is neither Jew nor Greek, there is neither slave nor free person, there is not male and female; for you are all one in Christ Jesus," the Christians of Galatia had been told (Galatians 3:28). Perhaps that is what some members of the crowd glimpsed, embodied by the two women, who stood together that day in the great arena of Carthage in the year 203.

Perpetua and Felicity were buried together in Carthage. In that city a great basilica was erected over the tomb that bore their names. Both canonized saints, their feast day is celebrated on March 7. What would you die for? Their lives continue to challenge us with that crucial question.

Questions for Reflection and Discussion

1. How would you define Perpetua's example?
2. What sustained her more than anything?
3. Was she motivated by faith—or egotism?
   Could she have been motivated by both?
4. Do you think her devotion to her faith outweighed her role as a mother? Could you make such a choice?
5. Was Perpetua's martyrdom self-glorifying or self- sacrificing?
6. Do you think she was "driven" or "called?"
   Could she have been both?
7. What can Perpetua's life teach us in our time?
8. Do we need Perpetua's kind of commitment today?
9. Would you have gone with Perpetua into the arena?
10. Where is "the moment of truth" for this heroine?

Teresa of Avila
(1515–1582)

The donkey cart jolted along another rutted road. The sole passenger, a black-veiled nun, gripped her seat. Tired and hungry, she was on mission yet again. Abruptly the cart overturned, spilling her into a river's muddy shallows. "Lord," she reportedly exclaimed, "if this is how you treat your friends, no wonder you have so few." Teresa of Avila had long been on intimate speaking terms with God.

"Prayer, in my view," she wrote, "is nothing but friendly inter-course, frequent solitary converse with him we know who loves us." With the years, her own prayer life had spiraled deeper, yielding mystical intervals when she felt God's love pierce her heart. This she described in her classic books on prayer, written amid her wide travels through Spain to found seventeen new convents. A daring spiritual trailblazer, Teresa defied traditional roles: as a woman, as a nun, and as a spiritual seeker. She managed to accomplish this in turbulent times, at risk of dire punishment by the dreaded Spanish Inquisition.

Born in a walled fortress city, Teresa was a passionate and re-bellious child. At the age of five, she decided that she should run away from home with her older brother. Stimulated by the tales of valiant Christian martyrs, she wanted to "go off to the land of the Moors and beg them, out of love of God, to cut off our heads there." Martyrdom for the faith seemed quite glorious to Teresa and Rodrigo.

An uncle intercepted the children, and Teresa never met the sacrificial death she had envisioned for herself. Indeed, her story lacks the overt drama of those who gave their lives for their faith. Instead, the drama of Teresa's life was played out on an internal level.

When she undertook this vocation, she boldly defied the standard beliefs of her day—women were not thought to be capable of a deep prayer life or spirituality. Teresa of Avila changed that perception forever. She also helped to legitimize a practice we take for granted: mental prayer.

At twenty, she ran away from her father's house and entered the convent of Avila. Once there, she could not understand why she sometimes experienced interior visions. As we have seen with Joan of Arc and others, private revelations were highly suspect by the Church. Teresa consulted many people about her internal life;

rumors of her mysticism spread. Some who heard the rumors suspected that Teresa's spiritual gifts came from demonic possession.

Still young, she turned to the wise Jesuit, Francis Borgia, who today is a saint. After listening carefully to his charge, Father Borgia offered consolation. He firmly determined that Teresa was the blessed recipient of authentic divine revelations. Freed from her fears, she began to see images of Christ in prayer. However, illness interfered with her vocation, and gradually she began to slip away from spiritual discipline.

By her own admission, Teresa's religious vocation grew perfunctory and passionless. At that time, her Carmelite Order had turned lax. It did not demand a simple, disciplined life but endorsed a leisurely, social pattern. In those times, nuns were often wealthy women who had maids and wore jewelry. In that era, it was believed that women were not intelligent enough to have a serious religious calling and a rich inner life.

It was not unusual for the sisters to conduct themselves like society matrons, spending hours entertaining their visitors in the parlors. In such an atmosphere, mental prayer was difficult. Teresa preferred gossip to spirituality in this phase of her vocational life. A delightful conversationalist, she turned from the silence needed for recollection and prayer and did what was expected—for a while.

Charming, attractive, and lively, Teresa had a natural gift for the sociable life. She went on in this way for nineteen years. And then, Teresa of Avila reached her own watershed moment. After nearly two decades, she found herself faced with a definitive choice: continue as a charming but "lukewarm" nun—or completely commit herself to an intense, intimate, and demanding spiritual life.

An unexpected conversion experience changed everything. One day, Teresa was suddenly drawn to a statue depicting the crucified Christ. All at once, Teresa felt overwhelmed by Jesus' self-sacrifice.

As she meditated on the statue, a sense of divine love seemed to flood her. How had she come to drift so far from God? She knew she needed to change her life's focus—and her convent's focus, as well. Teresa had no doubt about women's intelligence or spiritual depths.

For Teresa of Avila, the "tipping point" of her life was clear. She may have longed for a renewed faith-commitment on a deep level, invisible even to herself. Or she may have experienced a sudden spiritual call in the tradition of Saint Paul on the Damascus road. Whatever the exact circumstances of Teresa's watershed moment, it led to clarity, commitment, and constancy for her life.

Teresa of Avila surpassed even those goals. She became one of the greatest masters of spirituality in the Christian tradition. Her reawakening can hearten us all—and show us how her faith's support carried her indomitably through a series of great challenges. Ironically, one of these arose from Teresa's own Order.

The Carmelite Order's original rule had emphasized quiet, simplicity, and regular times of prayer. But these rules had become lax; almost lost. Teresa understood all too well how easily one could be distracted from God's presence; this had been her own experience for years. Now her sense of God's presence brought her such joy, she longed to share it with her sisters. "Prayer is an act of love," she later wrote. "Learn to see God in the details of your life, for he is everywhere."

Teresa saw that she must encourage her Carmelite sisters in a simpler external life that would cultivate the inner life of prayer. She must take a daring step. Somehow, she must reform her Order and return it to its original focus. That was her calling: reform for the sake of true spirituality. Whatever the price, Teresa knew she must persevere.

This was a weighty and risky undertaking; Teresa's conscience was leading her to defy her Order's superiors, her Church's hierarchy, and many who preferred the more comfortable status quo. She would have to raise funds as well—an unseemly occupation for a nun, some thought.

Even so, Teresa defied convention and followed her sense of divine calling. Finally she received permission to begin fund-raising and in this endeavor, her natural charm and wit won over many donors. The first of her new convents was consecrated in 1562 at Avila. There she encountered strong opposition—from her own Order, from her own neighbors, and from the Church itself.

She might have stopped there. She might have taken a rest. She might have taken the times into consideration. The feared Spanish Inquisition had gained power and struck homes without warning. Even inadvertent "heresies" were punished and "irregular beliefs" were often punished with imprisonment, torture, or death.

Teresa's own confessor, John of the Cross, had a holy and devout soul, but even he had run afoul of the Inquisition. His penalty was a long imprisonment in a dungeon in Toledo. There, through his own experience, John had developed his famous term "the dark night of the soul," still a hallmark of Christian spirituality. For Teresa, too, there could be peril if she continued with her reform, guided by "private revelations." These were particularly suspect in the eyes of the Inquisition. And yet, her conscience would not allow her to deny her personal religious convictions.

Teresa's intentions were not applauded. In fact, she was publicly reprimanded from the pulpit of her own parish church. Her own sisters felt a sense of betrayal. The specter of the Inquisition arose again. An investigation was instigated by her own town of Avila. Teresa must have known that change was threatening—but she also knew what God was asking her to do.

Teresa's desire was aligned with the divine will: Just as she needed a simple life of prayer, so did her community. With this certainty, she had the courage to defy all fear of the Inquisition. "Let nothing disturb you, let nothing frighten you," she wrote. "All things are passing, God never changes. Patient endurance attains all things...God alone suffices." Her courage was founded on her faith, now a steady fire within her. This faith was reinforced by her ongoing visionary experiences, detailed in her books on spirituality: These are still widely read and valued today as guides to a deeper life of prayer.

The Interior Castle and *The Way of Perfection* speak across denominational and cultural lines, guiding the reader through various stages of the soul's inner life. These works are considered to be of the same stature of such spiritual classics as Saint Augustine's *Confessions*.

Her writings abound in accessible guidance on the art of prayer: "the important thing is not to think much," she wrote, "but to love much and so do whatever awakens your love." For her written works alone, Teresa is admired as a spiritual master , although her books came under the scrutiny of the sixteenth century's Spanish Inquisition. Teresa had tasted the "prayer of quiet," an overwhelming sense of God's peace, and she had known the "prayer of union" when she felt herself melting into God's very self.

Teresa herself was not impressed with her famous spiritual raptures. She leavened her obvious holiness with her natural humor. "May God protect me from gloomy saints," she would say. She was always open to God, whatever the guise the divine took. A story tells of Teresa rushing around, overly busy with her convent's tasks. Suddenly she noticed a small boy at the foot of the stairs. "Who are you?" he asked her. "I am Teresa of Jesus," she replied. "Who are you?" The boy answered, "I am Jesus of Teresa," and disappeared.

One of her visions captured the imagination of the famed sculptor Bernini. His renowned work, *The Ecstasy of Saint Teresa,* can still be viewed at the church of Santa Maria della Vittoria in Rome. The sculpture is based on Teresa's own description of a special mystical experience which only came to her once in her life.

She saw an angel with a "long spear of gold, and at the iron's point there seemed to be a little fire. He appeared to me to be thrusting it at times into my heart...and to leave me all on fire with a great love of God. The pain was so great that it made me moan; and yet so surpassing was the sweetness of this excessive pain that I could not wish to be rid of it...." Naturally, Teresa never forgot this revelation and it inspired her for the rest of her life.

Despite her wisdom, Teresa was at risk. She was a visionary in an age when personal mysticism was zealously questioned. She was a reformer at a time when the traditions of the Church were fiercely guarded. And, most risky of all, she was a woman exercising extraordinary authority in an era when women's roles were strictly limited. Even so, she refused to deny her mystical experiences. Whatever the cost, she felt she must be true to her beliefs.

Teresa's father, a prosperous merchant, had a certain social standing which may have been protective. He had bought a title and married into the aristocracy long before. Teresa's grandfather, however, had been a Jewish *converso*, choosing Catholicism over exile in 1492. This fact could be used against Teresa if anyone wanted to cast aspersions on her own orthodoxy or simply make trouble for her.

And yet, Teresa's deep sense of calling outweighed any sense of personal danger. She would need all her wisdom and faith for the challenges ahead. Her pioneering vocation placed her under suspicion by the Spanish Inquisition. In addition, Teresa was attacked by the older, more liberal sector of the Carmelite Order. Enemies of her reforming work denounced her to the Spanish Inquisition. The "definitors" of the Order, in a solemn collection of resolutions, denied Teresa permission to found any more convents.

She was placed under a form of "house arrest" at her convent dedicated to Saint Joseph at Toledo. For three years, Teresa complied with this order—but not deferentially or silently. Had she chosen a secure position, her reforming work might have ended in Toledo. However, Teresa risked greater punishment by writing protest letters to King Philip II and a detailed autobiography.

Through this remarkable autobiography Teresa acquitted herself admirably in the eyes of the Inquisition and fared far better than her spiritual advisor, John of the Cross. In the end, events did not turn on her father's title or her own revelations; her own words were her salvation

At last, in 1579, the Spanish Inquisition formally ceased all investigations of Teresa. At the request of Pope Gregory XIII, a provincial, or supervisor, was appointed for Teresa's reformed Order, and the king formed a special board to protect it. Immediately, Teresa went into action, founding four more convents. The last one, established in 1582, was located in the city of Grenada. Teresa's "Constitution," set down by her in the 1560s, stipulated poverty as one of the basic conditions of the reformed Carmelite's life, along with the wearing of sandals instead of fine leather shoes. Teresa's "Constitution" continues to guide male and female Carmelites today.

Several Dominican and Jesuit priests were able to discern God's work in Teresa's soul—not the devil's. She herself knew how to discern the origins of her visions. Peace was a fruit of God's presence, as was inspiration. "If these effects are not present," she wrote, "I would greatly doubt that the raptures come from God; on the contrary I would fear lest they be caused by rabies." In the end, she was cleared to found more reformed convents—seventeen in all. This she did for most of her life, recording her experiences in *The Book of Foundations*: a remarkable guide to the workings of Carmelite communities and in use to this day.

Teresa of Avila died on one of her journeys and was buried at her convent at Alba de Tormes in Salamanca. There, the Convent of the Annunciation is the foremost shrine to honor Teresa. She was beatified in 1614 by Pope Paul V and canonized in 1622 by Pope Gregory XV. Teresa is one of the patron saints of Spain. In 1970 she became the first woman to be honored with the title Doctor of the Church.

Instead of becoming a martyr, her childhood dream, Teresa turned into something just as significant: a stellar guide to the interior castle of our souls where God always waits.

Questions for Reflection and Discussion

1. How would you define Teresa of Avila's example?
2. What sustained her more than anything?
3. Was she motivated by faith—or anger?
   Could she have been motivated by both?
4. How do you feel about Teresa's visionary side?
   Does it put you off or interest you?
5. Why did she defy her Order and reform it?
6. Do you think she was "driven" or "called?"
   Could she have been both?
7. Do you believe religious life should be simple?
8. How would you have faced the Spanish Inquisition
   as a woman and a mystic?
9. Would you defy your own community to reform it?
10. Where is "the moment of truth" for this heroine?

Elizabeth Seton of Emmitsburg (1774–1821)

"How dare you?" She could almost hear them spit the words. The tailor had turned her down. The butcher had turned her away. The shop girl had turned her back. "Papist, papist," they were probably thinking. They might as well have hissed, "Traitor." Of course Elizabeth had been warned; her Anglican pastor at Trinity Church knew this would happen.

When she had left his faith for another, Elizabeth Seton had crossed an invisible boundary line—one that divided natives from immigrants, servants from masters, poor from well-to-do. In New York City in 1805, no one who was anyone was Catholic. No one who was anyone hired them, married them, or dined with them. And of course, it went without saying: No one who was anyone became a Catholic. That was absolutely unthinkable.

"How dare you?" Elizabeth could remember her family's scandalized faces when she spoke of her conversion. Her sister Mary, her brother-in-law, Wright...all of them. How could Elizabeth abandon the family tradition, going back to French Huguenots? How could she put herself in a position to be scorned, rejected, shunned by society? And how could she follow that despised religion itself: ritualized, romantic—Roman? That "sect" simply had no place in American society. Until 1789, New York State had outlawed Catholicism. It was a faith for the illiterate, the ignorant, the indigent. Elizabeth was none of those things. How, then, could she select it? It was a matter of conscience, Elizabeth might have said. It was a matter of the heart. It was a matter of God's call to her spirit. But how could she really explain? She was weary of argument and worn-out with worry. At twenty-nine, Elizabeth Bayley Seton was an impoverished widow and mother of five. If she did not reverse her religious stand, her family would not help her. They had offered no financial aid since her conversion. It was spiritual blackmail, nothing less—and Elizabeth would not give in to it. Instead, she strengthened her resolve. Let her relatives think her selfish. True, she had dared to make this choice at a crucial time.

Perhaps she had not realized how costly a choice it was. Elizabeth must get on in a world that hated her religion. Her conversion had ensured that people would ostracize her and her children. Her little school, just started, quickly failed. People were suspicious of

Elizabeth, fearing she would try to convert their sons. She had to sell her "household effects" at public auction.

Now she scandalized her family by running a boarding house, taking in all manner of transients who often could not pay. To make matters worse, Elizabeth had been accused of "corrupting" her niece with "pope-ish" doctrine. For this, Elizabeth faced a deportation order from the state Senate itself.

Before any action could be taken, Advent had turned into Christmas Eve. With her children, Elizabeth walked through the cold to Barclay Street, home to small, rundown Saint Peter's, the only Catholic church in the city.

Accustomed to beautiful sanctuaries, Elizabeth was still adjusting to the plainness of Saint Peter's. Its parishioners were poor; the women wore scarves on their heads, not bonnets, and few men had warm coats on this chilly night. Even so, Elizabeth felt peace come over her as she stepped inside. The nave was flickering with votive candles and everywhere was the smell of tallow, flowers, incense, and simple greenery near the Christmas crib.

As Midnight Mass unfolded, Elizabeth's sense of peace grew— until she heard the scuffling and shouts from outside. It was in the silence after Holy Communion that she could make out the angry words: "Papist trash, Roman scum." The voices grew louder; boots stamped nearer. Elizabeth's children trembled against her. She did not need to tell them what was happening. They knew. "*Ite, Missa est*," Father O'Brien ended the mass. "*Deo gratias*." The congregation's reply was nearly eclipsed by the shouts of the mob encircling the church. Would they storm it? Burn it? Throw rocks through its windows? Elizabeth must have held her children and prayed.

Suddenly Father O'Brien's Irish face hovered above Elizabeth. He told her that Mayor Clinton was there; the constables had arrived. No one wanted a fire in the city on Christmas Eve. Even so, it would be best to get the women and children out of the sanctuary. Frightened, they would not move. The priest was asking Elizabeth to lead the exodus from Saint Peter's. Well-respected as she was, the women were sure to follow her out.

Gathering her children, she stepped into the aisle. She took one step, then another. Behind her she heard other footfalls. At the church doors, she paused, then opened them. Outside there was a blur of torchlight.

With her children clinging to her cloak, Elizabeth walked into the stinging air of Christmas morning.

Later, in their boarding house rooms, she let each child open one small present. Small they were, this year: a tin whistle, hair ribbons, a spool of bright thread. Gradually, the children drifted into sleep. The streets were quiet. Elizabeth remained awake, on watch, all the same. Despite herself, she must have recalled other Christmas Eves: the excitement, many gifts, joyous greetings. Ten years earlier, she had just given birth to her first child. Twenty years earlier, as a child herself, she had cheered the Broadway procession of General George Washington, hero of the Revolutionary War.

Of course, that was before the Seton fortune had been lost. That was before Willy had died in Italy. *It was those Italians who won you over, wasn't it?* Elizabeth could imagine her godmother snapping out that sentence. Perhaps, in a way, this was true.

It really began when Willy became so ill with "The Seton Complaint." Consumption ran in his family, along with wit, grace, music, and a total disregard for financial matters. His father's business had lost ships at sea, that was true, but as her husband sickened, she had studied the ledgers and books on his desk. The business was nearly bankrupt.

There was only a little to go on with—and a little for a voyage to Italy, where the sunny climate might improve Willy's health. The family's friends and business associates, the Filicchis, would host them while the children stayed with Willy's sister. It was a desperate measure, as Elizabeth must have known.

The voyage was long and when the ship docked in Livorno, the Setons were held for weeks in quarantine. Their quarters were damp and chilly; Willy's cough worsened. Finally, they were released, but Willy was too ill to go far. On December 17, 1803, he died at Pisa, and the Filicchi family came to support Elizabeth. With her oldest daughter, Anna Maria, she was invited to stay at the Filicchis' estate in Livorno, on the beautiful southwest coast of Italy. Her hosts consoled her as she grieved and took her on restorative trips.

One, to Florence, made a deep impression on Elizabeth and she stood for a long time at the street-corner shrines. As she joined the Filicchis for worship, she felt strangely moved—and oddly comforted. Her attraction to Catholicism intensified until she knew that she could not go on without it. This, she saw, was her way to God. She had never known anything like this peace before.

It was then that Elizabeth Bayley Seton must have reached her own "moment of truth." As she knelt in a Livorno church, she left a bouquet behind—a symbol of her commitment to her new spiritual path. This path, she knew, would evoke shock and even horror from her family and friends.

It would drastically change her life and the lives of her children. In the long run, it would also change the American faith-tradition of her choice.

In the short term, this move would lead her away from familiar comforts. Her decision was not impulsive but carefully explored and deeply felt. It was the toughest choice of Elizabeth Seton's life. A single mother, a widow with low funds, and five children, Elizabeth opted to follow her conscience rather than comfort. One wonders if she feared for her decision's impact on her children. Perhaps her faith overcame her fear. And she would certainly need that faith when she returned to her American world.

Of course, when Elizabeth returned to New York, everyone was appalled by her "notions." Even so, she went ahead with the steps toward conversion. Ostracized and abandoned by family and friends, she dared to follow her conscience and her convictions. On Ash Wednesday, March 14, 1805, she was received into the Catholic Church at Saint Peter's.

Eleven days later, on the Feast of the Annunciation, Elizabeth made her first Communion. Her joy was close to overflowing; her isolation was nearly complete. As New York City grew more hostile, Elizabeth contemplated a move—mostly for her children's sake.

The first Catholic bishop of America, John Carroll of Maryland, was instrumental in the Setons' relocation to Baltimore, which was founded by a Catholic and long known for religious tolerance to all. Thanks to the Filicchi family, her sons would attend Georgetown College in Washington, D.C.

Through Father Dubourg from Saint Mary's Seminary, Elizabeth Seton opened another school, in Baltimore, this one for girls—and this time, a success. Bishop Carroll was a wise man, aware of the tremendous opposition to his faith in America. He realized that Elizabeth Seton broke the negative stereotypes of Catholics, however unfair they were. She was well-born, well-spoken, well-educated. She would be a superb choice as the founder of the first order of nuns in this new nation. Meanwhile, other women were drawn to Elizabeth Seton's way of life. It was the life of a teaching sister, and it appealed to many young Catholics with no vocational avenues open to them.

But what of her children? Elizabeth Seton faced a very modern dilemma, torn between her vocation and her family. After much prayer and reflection, she felt God was calling her to both. She would be both Mother and Mama. Privately and quietly, Elizabeth took her vows as a nun before Bishop Carroll and her eldest daughter. But Elizabeth would not be staying in Baltimore, she learned.

Another aristocratic convert to Catholicism, Samuel Sutherland Cooper, admired Elizabeth Seton and the effort to form an American foundation. A member of the wealthy Virginia gentry, Cooper contributed what was an immense sum in 1809: $10,000. This fortune was offered to purchase a tract of farmland in Emmitsburg, Maryland, for the new order and a school for poor children.

Like later West-bound pioneers, Elizabeth and eighteen sisters set out for the wilderness of Emmitsburg by covered wagon. By 1810, the new community was quartered in a large log cabin with multiple fireplaces.

There was no need for added austerities. Life, that first year, was challenging. At times, in winter, snow filtered through cracks in the cabin's roof and dusted the sisters' faces as they slept.

Elizabeth Bayley Seton was elected mother superior of this new Order, the Daughters of Charity of Saint Joseph. She would go on to lay the foundations for a nationwide system of free Catholic schools, orphanages, hospitals, nurseries, and homes for lepers. In eleven years, Mother Seton's Order had established itself in some twenty locations. Hers was a "celestial commission," a priest told her.

A personal crisis shook Mother Seton in 1812. Her eldest daughter, Anna Maria, died of consumption at sixteen. "After Anna was taken," her mother wrote, "I was so often expecting to lose my senses, and my head was so disordered that unless for the daily duties always before me, I did not know much of what I did or what I had left undone." Her despair over this beloved child must have reopened the wounds left from Willy's death. As always, however, Mother Seton's deep faith sustained her, and her intimacy with God increased. Her devotion was well-known to her Order and she became a gifted spiritual guide. When her youngest daughter,

Rebecca, died in 1816, also from consumption, Mother Seton's faith deepened again through her grief.

Still, the Order continued to grow. The original school at Emmitsburg flourished and many Daughters of Charity were also able to work among the poor. In 1814, the Order opened an orphanage in Philadelphia, and in 1817, another was founded in New York. Somehow, Mother Seton found time to translate the Life of Saint Vincent de Paul, in addition to maintaining a wide correspondence and several diaries; these show her intense sense of God's presence, experienced through her devotional nature. It has been remarked that her maternal demeanor was helpful to her community, as was her humility. In the original Emmitsburg chapel, Mother Seton's favorite place is marked on the altar rail—not "center stage" but far to one side, almost next to the wall.

In 1819, Mother Seton was elected superior of her community for the third time. By then she knew that she, too, was suffering from "the Seton Complaint" that had taken such a heavy toll on her family. She called this vote of confidence "the election of the dead," perhaps using her characteristic good nature to lighten a serious mood. She remained active as long as she could and even from her sickbed, she continued with writing and administrative details.

On January 4, 1821, Mother Elizabeth Seton died in her room at Emmitsburg, with her daughter Catherine at her side. Mother Seton was forty-seven. She could not know that within twenty-five years, a flood of Catholic immigrants would arrive in America—and the network she founded would be waiting for them.

Mother Seton also left two sons and a daughter. At twenty-three, Richard was lost at sea. William, the eldest son, also joined the Navy but survived his brother by forty years. Catherine, the middle daughter became a devoted nun, worked tirelessly for prison reform, and died at ninety years of age. At its peak, in 1911, the Daughters of

Charity numbered about six thousand. Mother Seton was beatified in 1963 and canonized on September 14, Holy Cross Day, in 1975. She is the first American-born saint to be so honored.

Reflection on Mother Seton's life reveals important themes. For her, a life of comfort and privilege was not enough; a life of spiritual depth was more important to her. This is a motif that recurs in other faith-based narratives. A daughter of privilege, Elizabeth could have had ample financial and emotional support after her husband's early death. Her willingness to sacrifice such support shows the strength of her religious convictions.

One might wonder about the effect these convictions may have had upon her children, however. In-depth research for *Miracles: A Novel Based on the Life of Mother Elizabeth Seton*, does not uncover any detrimental effects on her sons and daughters. Two of these daughters were victims of the family vulnerability to tuberculosis, which would have manifested itself in any case. The two Seton sons were well-educated and well-launched in the world, although Richard was tragically young when he died at sea. Daughter Catherine enjoyed a long and fruitful life.

One sees the constant balancing that Mother Seton had to do to maintain her vocation and her family life. The tension between the two roles continues to resonate with the situations of twenty-first-century women. In that way, Mother Seton's life is pertinent to today's challenges for Catholics and non-Catholics alike. The recurring theme of personal sacrifice is paramount here.

Another important and recurring theme is religious freedom. One notes the prevalence of religious prejudice and even murderous hostility in many stories of personal courage. The reaction of Mother Seton's family to her conversion challenges our own standards of tolerance. Instead of seeing a convert as a "traitor," we may ask ourselves how open we are to an individual's right to follow God's calling. That mandate remains a choice and a challenge for us today.

As noted, from 1845 onward, there was an unprecedented tide of Catholic immigrants to America. Just a quarter-century after Mother Seton's death, the potato crop failed in Ireland, plunging that country's Catholic population into the Great Famine. Millions of Irish Catholic immigrants flooded American cities. Although their suffering was intense, it was greatly ameliorated by the institutions put in place by the Daughters of Charity.

Mother Seton's Order had twenty-five years to grow before its presence was drastically needed. In hindsight, its existence may seem coincidental—or providential. As a Protestant and as a Catholic, Mother Seton's unquestionable devotion to God unites the two great streams of faith that have shaped America.

....

Questions for Reflection and Discussion

1. Does Elizabeth Seton's example inspire you? Why? Why not?
2. What sustained her more than anything?
3. Was she motivated by faith—or anguish?
   Could she have been motivated by both?
4. Was her mission fair to her children?
5. Was Mother Seton's conversion an act of conscience?
   Why? Why not?
6. Do you think she was "desperate" or "called?"
   Could she have been both?
7. Do you think Mother Seton was right to break
   with her family's faith?
8. Do we need Mother Seton's kind of conscience today?
9. Would you break away from family tradition to worship
   according to your own beliefs?
10. Where is "the moment of truth" for this heroine?

Florence Nightingale of London (1820-1910)

"I can stand out a war with any man," Florence Nightingale wrote from the British army hospital in Scutari, Turkey.

The fabled "Lady With the Lamp" had a commander's will and a mystic's spirit. The soldiers saw her as a ministering angel. The hospital's chief saw her as trouble. An early biographer wrote: "She was not 'the lady with the lamp.' She was the lady with the brain—one of those rare personalities who reshape the contours of life."

Florence Nightingale, the founder of modern nursing, is not generally known for her private spirituality. And yet her remarkable life of service is rooted in a consistent sense of religious vocation. After one of her mystical experiences, she wrote, "God called me... and asked if I would do good for him, for him, without the reputation." And early on she resolved "to think only of God."

At sixteen, while walking alone on the grounds of her father's vast estate, Florence was overwhelmed by an extraordinary sense of divine communion. "On February 7th, 1837, God spoke to me and called me to his service," she wrote in her diary that evening in her well-appointed bed chamber.

Florence Nightingale experienced the grace of revelation, as did Joan of Arc. However, both women were called to missions that were unclear. Although their mysticism signaled their special calling to a commitment, they had to wait for years before they understood what form that commitment would take.

While Florence Nightingale waited, she prepared herself with learning, with training, and with sacrifice of a love relationship. When the time was right, she was able to meet the tremendous challenge of the British hospital at Scutari, in the Crimea. Her earlier revelations must have provided Nightingale with great strength to upset every expectation of her family and class.

Florence's background was wealthy and privileged. Her bent was mathematical. Her father was a Unitarian and an intellectual. Her destiny was to marry well. Florence Nightingale defied her family, class, convention, suitors and society to follow an undefined divine calling. It would be several years, however, before she understood what she was meant to do for God.

Meanwhile, she went through the motions demanded by her mother: an endless round of parties, dances, fittings, and teas. These bored her to tears. However, Florence turned down all marriage proposals and continued to wait on God's will for her. Although she fell in love with Richard Monckton-Milnes, Baron Houghton, she refused him. It was her belief that her calling would demand total dedication—and celibacy. "To be nailed to a continuation and exaggeration of my present life," she wrote, "without the hope of another would be intolerable to me."

When she could get away from social obligations, Florence visited sick cottagers near Embley Park and the Nightingales' summer home, Lea Hurst. She also studied books on medicine and hospital administration.

After watching a pauper die in a workhouse infirmary, her sense of direction began to clarify. The sight of that death made an indelible impression on her. In 1844, Florence began to advocate better healthcare in such "infirmaries." These were not places for ladies to visit, Florence was told. The women who worked there were poor, or alcoholic, or harlots. This did not matter to Florence. By now she had discerned her vocation. It far surpassed the customs of her class. If her vocation meant defiance of custom, Florence was willing to take that stand.

Her conscience prompted her to make a shocking decision. In 1845, she informed her family that she wanted to become a nurse. Mrs. Nightingale was devastated and outraged. Her husband forbade his daughter to pursue the matter further. Refusing to give up her call, Florence watched and waited for new opportunities.

Always a realist, Florence came to accept this hard fact: she would never have the approval of her own family. It is seldom noted that support and help came to her from an unexpected source: Dr. Elizabeth Blackwell, the first woman to become an American physician. The two women met at Saint Bartholomew's Hospital in London and shared experiences. Blackwell had also defied conventional expectations of women and had faced down many obstacles to become a doctor. She urged Florence to persevere.

Her friends, Charles and Selina Bracebridge, introduced Florence to Sidney Herbert, recently the secretary of war. A man of influence and power, he was a fine partner to his wife and an equally fine mentor to Florence. Herbert was to play an important role in her professional life, and he was one of her few supporters as her calling unfolded.

Looking back, Florence would see the timing, on a larger scale, was just right. She felt God leading her forward again. Florence understood the movement within her own spirit. "For what is mysticism?" she wrote. "Is it not the attempt to draw near to God, not by rites or ceremonies, but by inward disposition? Is it not merely a hard word for 'The Kingdom of Heaven is within?' Heaven is neither a place nor a time."

In 1850, Florence began the active phase of her ministry. She traveled to Germany's respected medical Institution at Kaiserswerth. There, Lutheran deaconesses were trained as nurses under the guidance of Pastor Theodor Fliedner. Florence entered his program to learn more about working with the sick and the injured.

This, she later wrote, was the turning point of her life. Kaiserswerth coupled her two great commitments: medicine and spirituality. "I left Kaiserswerth feeling so brave, as if nothing could vex me again," she wrote. During Florence's intensive training, she gained a great deal of technical knowledge as well as skill in pastoral ministrations. The first of her many publications, brought out in 1851, was titled *The Institution of Kaiserswerth on the Rhine, for the Practical Training of Deaconesses.*

Her mission continued to take concrete form. "I still feel," she wrote, "that it is such a blessing to have been called, however unworthy, to be 'the handmaid of the Lord.'" At the age of thirty-three, Florence might have been considered a spinster. She saw herself quite differently. A new life was opening to her when she found her first professional position.

Through a series of connections, she became superintendent of a small charity hospital in Harley Street, the medical nexus of London. With her father's financial support, Florence was able to continue at the Institute for the Care of Sick Gentlewomen. Here, she gained further knowledge of nursing and administration, both of which would soon prove to be invaluable.

Her habit of defiance would also serve Florence Nightingale well as she faced a far greater series of challenges when the Crimean War broke out in 1854. Britain was allied with Turkey against Russia, and thousands of soldiers were sent to the front. Foreign correspondents began to penetrate the British army's lines, and respected newspapers shocked their readers with horrifying details. Britain's soldiers were sustaining severe causalities, and the wounded had overwhelmed the military medical facilities. The situation was especially acute at the vast hospital, once a barracks, at Scutari in Turkey.

Under the auspices of Sidney Herbert, Florence Nightingale felt called to lead a band of English nurses into service at the Scutari facility. Its location was strategic—just across the Black Sea from Balaklava, the center of British operations in the Crimea. Scutari's hospital was clearly in crisis, though Florence could not yet comprehend its extent. "If there is a hell on earth," she later wrote, "surely this is it...That this is the Kingdom of Hell, no one can doubt."

Florence never hesitated to use her resources or connections if these could serve her cause. With the assistance of contacts at the War Office, she was authorized to select thirty-eight women to travel with her to Turkey. After a long and complicated journey, the Nightingale party reached the overcrowded hospital on November 4, 1854. A major battle was about to send more wounded soldiers to the facility.

The chief of medical operations at Scutari, Dr. John Hall, openly resented Florence Nightingale and her nurses. He did not believe that the long tradition of male nurses should be broken by women. This, to him, was unseemly and insulting to the military. He and Florence instantly clashed, and this animosity continued. Hall saw the steely strength behind her feminine presence; she saw him as an obstructionist to the care of the wounded. It is also likely that Hall did not want the well-connected Miss Nightingale to see the ghastly conditions at his hospital. When she asked for a tour of the facility, Hall handed her a lantern and only permitted her to view the wards in the dark of night.

Walking four miles of corridors, Florence Nightingale saw enough. The filthy barracks housed hundreds of men in unventilated space, allowing a strong stench to permeate the air. The men lay unwashed, still bloody, many of them dead or dying. A contemporary observer describes Scutari as a "vast field of suffering and misery." Sheets, bandages, and shirts were in short supply or absent altogether.

No blankets covered the patients, and no laundries existed to clean their linens. Cholera and typhus were rampant under such conditions and caused even more fatalities than wounds sustained in battle. Florence remembered the emphasis on hygiene at Kaiserswerth and at a convent hospital she had visited in Alexandria. Even in the dimness, she recognized this situation for what it was: an absolute disgrace, breeding death.

Scutari's chaplain, the Reverend Sydney Osborne, was horrified by the absence of the commonest provision for the men once they got there...the scarcity of medicines, and the poor level of diet. Often, he observed, patients were served rations of raw meat. The entire scene was crawling with vermin.

Florence heard that shipments of foodstuffs simply did not turn up or were lost at sea. Using her own resources, she supplied the hospital with food, linens, and other necessities. These donations were met with a sense of resentment from the hospital staff.

Hall remained Florence's nemesis. In the face of such overwhelming challenges she might have given up and returned to England. Instead she wrote: "I am in sympathy with God, fulfilling the promise I came into the world for. What the disappointments of the conclusion of these six months no one can tell. But I am not dead, but alive." Frustrated, she retorted with a touch of sarcasm: "It may seem a strange principle to enunciate as the very first requirement of a hospital that it should do the sick no harm." Despite resistance from Dr. Hall and his staff, Florence set up a laundry, a kitchen, and began scrubbing down the dirt-encrusted floors.

After eight at night, the nurses were obligated to leave the wards to male orderlies. Florence, alone, walked the long corridors by lantern-light, pausing to speak to the soldiers. Moved by her ministrations, they began to watch for the "Lady With the Lamp." It was said that men would kiss her shadow as she passed. Florence never seemed impressed with the aura seen around her. Driven by her conscience and her calling, Florence's attention was drawn in many directions. "She's here, there, and everywhere," a former patient wrote. "You never lose sight of her."

Despite Hall's accusations, she avoided publicity and worked twenty hours a day. From her own words, Florence's supports were prayer and faith. "I never pray for anything temporal," she noted in her journal. "But when each morning comes, I kneel down before the rising sun and only say, 'behold the handmaid of the Lord—give me this day my work to do—no, not my work, but thine.'"

Continually checkmated by the military staff, Florence wrote a scathing letter to correspondent John Russell at *The London Times*. The letter exposed conditions at Scutari—and shocked Britain. Once the hospital's horrors were detailed in the English press, Florence began to make more headway. An open sewer lay underneath the wards, and the War Department dispatched a sanitary commission to remedy the situation.

Before the work was finished, the hospital's death rate was estimated at forty-two percent. During the hard winter of 1855, some two thousand men occupied the hospital, and nearly half of them perished there. Many of these died in Nightingale's arms. By June, however, the mortality figures had dropped significantly.

It was inevitable that Florence Nightingale would become run-down and susceptible to disease herself. As the situation at Scutari improved, she fell seriously ill with what was called "Crimea Fever." For nearly two weeks, her life was in danger. Across England and its battle stations, prayers were said for her recovery. Nightingale's own nurses cared for her, and after a difficult struggle, she emerged from the most dangerous phase of her illness.

Instead of resting, Florence returned to her work at Scutari, where she remained until March 1856. Still weak, she added another feature to her mission. In addition to her other duties, Florence attempted a reading program for the soldiers to add mental stimulation to her nursing program.

In August, after the war ended and the hospitals were shut down, Florence Nightingale finally went home to England. A hero's welcome awaited her, but Florence chose to slip unnoticed into the country and her family's Lea Hurst estate. Later that year, Queen Victoria invited Florence to Balmoral Castle for a royal audience.

Nightingale spoke at length with the royal couple about "everything that affects our present military hospital system." At the end of her audience, the queen presented Florence Nightingale with a brooch specially made for her. It was engraved with words from the Beatitudes: "Blessed are the merciful."

By 1860, Florence had raised some fifty thousand pounds to augment the Nightingale fund, in existence since 1855. This fund enabled her to establish the Nightingale Home for Nurses, a training facility which was the only institution to bear her name, at her request. Her physical strength never rebounded from her illness in the Crimea; poor health prevented her from functioning as superintendent of the new nursing school. Still, Florence oversaw the facility's growth and offered invaluable suggestions gleaned from her practical experience at Scutari.

Over the next years, she became reclusive and often limited by a variety of ailments. Still, Florence sent forth a steady stream of written works on many medical subjects, including hospital administration, hygiene, and her classic textbook, *Notes on Nursing*, which was considered the nurse's "bible" for decades. It went into several editions during and after Nightingale's long life.

Her books, reports, and pamphlets are credited with lowering peacetime hospital death rates, as well as those in wartime. Nightingale had made nursing a respectable occupation and raised it to the level of a profession. She was the first woman to be awarded the Order of Merit, which was presented to her in 1907. She received many other awards from numerous countries, but she continued her reclusive existence.

It is ironic that the "Lady With the Lamp" lived her last years in darkness. She lost her sight in the late 1890s and was herself nursed through her final decade. On August 13, 1910, she died peacefully in her sleep at her London residence. Her family was offered the use of Westminster Abbey for her funeral but her will requested a quiet ceremony at East Wellow, Hampshire, where her sister and parents were buried.

"The Lady With the Lamp" is best remembered from this report in *The London Times*: "She is a 'ministering angel' without any exaggeration in these hospitals, and as her slender form glides quietly along each corridor, every poor fellow's face softens with gratitude at the sight of her. When all the medical officers have retired for the night and silence and darkness have settled down upon those miles of prostrate sick, she may be observed alone with a little lamp in her hand, making her solitary rounds."

Questions for Reflection and Discussion

1. How would you characterize Florence Nightingale's legacy?
2. What sustained her more than anything?
3. Was she motivated by faith—or boredom?
   Could she have been motivated by both?
4. Her defiance upset her family—was it worth the cost?
5. Was Florence Nightingale's "mission" egocentric or heroic?
6. Do you think she was "driven" or "called?"
   Could she have been both?
7. What do you think about Nightingale's mysticism?
   Did it motivate her? How?
8. Do we need Florence Nightingale's kind of commitment today?
9. Would you give up a life of comfort for a life of service?
10. Where is "the moment of truth" for this heroine?

Dorothy Day of New York
(1897-1980)

"If I have achieved anything in my life, it is because I was not embarrassed to talk about God," Dorothy Day wrote. This sense of divine intimacy lasted, even when she raised eyebrows, controversy, criticism, and outright opposition.

Dorothy Day began as a radical who rejected religion and ended as a radical who embraced Christianity. In her early twenties, Dorothy was a Bohemian journalist, espousing left-wing causes and common-law marriage. By the time she was thirty and pregnant, she was irrevocably drawn back to God.

After an abortion years before, Dorothy had thought she would never have another child. Now, repentant and joyous, Dorothy struggled with her current relationship. Already involved with a nearby church, she defied Forster Batterham, an atheist, anarchist, and the father of her baby.

"How can there be no God," she demanded of Batterham, "when there are so many beautiful things?" Dorothy's change of heart ended their union.

She was determined to have her baby baptized. "I did not want my child to flounder as I had often floundered," Day wrote. "I wanted to believe, and I wanted my child to believe, and if belonging to a church would give her so inestimable a grace as faith in God, and the companionable love of the saints, then the thing to do was have her baptized a Catholic."

Day's daughter, Tamar, was born in March 1927 and by that year's end, mother and daughter had been received into the Church. In her book, *The Long Loneliness,* Day writes about the "natural happiness" she found in her commitment to Tamar and to God.

The way ahead was not easy, all the same. Dorothy, a single mother, reported on a hunger march in Washington, D.C., and found herself weeping at a church's altar rail. Stirred by the protestors, she agonized over a way to reconcile her political stance with her religious beliefs.

"I offered up a special prayer," she later said. "A prayer which came with tears and anguish, that some way would open up for me to use what talents I possessed for my fellow workers, for the poor."

The next day she returned to her New York apartment and met the man who would answer this prayer—and change Dorothy Day's life forever. His name was Peter Maurin, a French émigré and former Christian Brother. During twenty-five years of helping the poor, his existence resembled that of a mendicant friar. Celibate, free of possessions, devoted to prayer, Maurin was committed to social justice.

When he approached the editor of *Commonweal* magazine, he was handed Dorothy's address. Day's meeting with Maurin seemed providential. This eccentric wayfarer offered his hostess an inspired idea: to start a special kind of newspaper. This publication would feature the Gospel mandate, translating it into specific steps toward a just social order. Dorothy wholly committed herself to the plan.

Dorothy Day had made costly choices before. Perhaps the toughest was her decision to return to faith, bringing her daughter with her—and losing the father of her child in the process. Dorothy's heartfelt prayer for guidance marks another watershed moment, in which she relinquishes control of her life to God, so that the divine will might use her gifts. Her co-creation of the Catholic Worker Movement, with Peter Maurin, marks her most significant life-long commitment. At that point her life changes, her mission takes shape—and Dorothy Day accepts her calling.

This new effort, integrating her experience, gifts, and faith, appeared to answer her recent prayers. She immediately went into action, using her kitchen as her headquarters. The paper would be sold for a penny each, and the Paulist Press agreed to print over two thousand copies. On May Day, 1931, *The Catholic Worker* went on sale—and became a resounding success.

Seven months later, Day was printing one hundred thousand copies a month. The paper was different from any other—simultaneously religious and radical. It envisioned an improved social order, supported the labor movement, and invited its readers' honest responses. With Maurin as catalyst, Dorothy Day had created a new channel of expression for the working poor and made this newspaper accessible to all.

It also featured Maurin's prophetic essays. These urged a return to Christian hospitality for "the stranger"—the homeless, the hungry, the destitute. Instead of letting institutions care for such people, Peter Maurin believed in a "Christ Room," set aside in every house and every parish.

As winter came on, the homeless began to appear at Dorothy's apartment. Soon overcrowded and chaotic at first, Day's home became the first of what *The Catholic Worker* termed "houses of hospitality." These became one of the most visible signs of what became known as the Catholic Worker Movement.

At first, the guests in Day's houses were mostly men: "Gray men," she wrote, "the color of lifeless trees and bushes and winter soil, who had in them as yet none of the green of hope, the rising sap of faith." However, to the surprise of the men, no Catholic Worker house tried to convert or reform anyone. A crucifix was the only religious emblem on the wall.

By 1936, the movement had gone national, with thirty-three "houses of hospitality" springing up around the country. These shelters appeared in America at a time of great need, during the Great Depression. However, the movement was not universally accepted or applauded. Many voiced the sentiment that Catholic Worker "clients" should get jobs like other poor people. Most of Dorothy's guests, however, were broken people with problems that kept them off the job market. "They live with us, they die with us and we give them a Christian burial...," Day told a social worker.

"Once they are taken in, they become members of the family. Or rather, they were always members of the family. They are our brothers and sisters in Christ." The Catholic Worker Movement continued to flourish. It soon extended to the slums and farmlands of Canada and Great Britain and firmly took root. Today there are more than one hundred "houses of hospitality," from Australia to Germany, Mexico to Sweden, serving the homeless, the indigent, and the hungry.

Dorothy Day had traveled a long way from her Bohemian youth. Perhaps that phase of her life taught her a certain detachment from material things. When she had frequented the cafés of Greenwich Village with Eugene O'Neill, she had supported herself on slender means. Refusing her father's financial support, she had cultivated the practice of simplicity. Throughout her life, she bought all her clothes from discount stores and thrift shops. This habitual frugality served her well as she continued with her dedicated vocation.

Instead of writing about Socialist issues, Dorothy was living out her earlier passion for social justice. Now, however, this vision was firmly based on her devotion to Christ and his gospel. Like others who dedicated their lives to the poor, she often quoted Matthew 25—that ministering to the "least of these," Jesus said, was ministry to him. This text was always important to Day; so important that it is easy to forget that she grew up in Brooklyn and Chicago without any strong religious influence.

Dorothy expanded her commitment to Gospel values in other ways. She rented several rural properties as farming communities that gradually changed into houses of hospitality. Among them was the Maryfarm Retreat House in Newburgh, New York, and the Peter Maurin Farm on Staten Island, which branched out into the Hudson Valley.

For Dorothy, however, this still was not enough; her conscience would not let her stop there. She believed that nonviolence and pacifism were essential parts of the message of Jesus. This view provoked far more controversy than her network of Catholic Worker houses. The Catholic Church had supported wars and crusades; the only major dissenting voice had belonged to Saint Francis of Assisi.

With the outbreak of the Spanish Civil War in 1936, pacifism became a major issue for the Catholic Worker Movement. Catholic leaders supported the Fascists, led by Francisco Franco, but Dorothy Day declined to take any official position on the war. This angered many American bishops and other Catholics; her newspaper's readership dropped dramatically. Even so, when the United States entered World War II, she held to her pacifist stance—a highly unpopular position. Several members of her movement departed, and fifteen "houses of hospitality" had to close.

Dorothy stayed true to her conscience. *The Catholic Worker* continued to support pacifism. "Our manifesto is the Sermon on the Mount," she wrote, adding a statement of loyalty to America. "We have been the only country in the world where men and women of all nations have taken refuge from oppression." She urged her movement's followers to dedicate their energies to the sick, the wounded, the hungry, and "our works of mercy in our houses and on our farms." Dorothy Day was not intimidated by opposition. "The servant is not greater than the master," she often reminded her followers.

Christ had suffered—why should his disciples expect less? After the end of World War II, the Catholic Worker Movement boycotted New York State's civil defense drills. "In the name of Jesus, who is God, who is love," Dorothy Day declared in a leaflet. "We will not obey this order to pretend, to evacuate, to hide. We will not be drilled into fear. We do not have faith in God if we depend on the Atom Bomb."

She considered her nonviolent dissent as a penance for the bombing of Japan in 1945. When she repeated this act of civil disobedience again and again, she was repeatedly jailed. After Day criticized Francis Cardinal Spellman of New York, the Archdiocese distanced itself from Dorothy for a time, urging her to expunge the word "Catholic" from her newspaper's name. The name remained unchanged, and Dorothy Day continued with her pacifist stance.

In 1963, she joined fifty "Mothers for Peace" in Rome, hoping for an official Vatican statement opposing warfare. She visited Rome again in 1965 for a hunger strike to benefit this hope. As a result of the fast, and other efforts, the Second Vatican Council condemned any act of war "directed to the indiscriminate destruction of whole cities or vast areas with their inhabitants. In addition, the council also urged that "conscientious objectors" be legally recognized by their respective countries.

During the Vietnam War, Dorothy Day participated in many non-violent protests—and went to jail for her beliefs. Many remember the spare and straight-spined Dorothy saying her rosary on picket lines. This image integrates Day's radical stands on social issues with her orthodox Catholic devotion.

Some called her a Socialist, even a Communist. These accusations did not bother her. However, she vehemently protested when she was called a saint. "When they call you a saint," she often said, "it means basically that you're not to be taken seriously." Day took her calling quite seriously to the end of her life. She demanded a great deal from herself: a laywoman who followed the monastic vows of poverty, chastity, and obedience, while constantly active in the world. She never gave up her first commitment to the poor around her.

At seventy-five, she was jailed again for participating in an illegal protest on behalf of impoverished farm workers. By then, her physical strength was beginning to wane, but her spiritual strength remained as strong as ever. Dorothy gave fifty-five years to her causes, her conscience, and her God. If that meant controversy and condemnation, she was never deterred. She was entirely serious about her beliefs and the dictates of her conscience, even if that meant controversy and costly condemnation.

"Neither revolutions nor faith is won without keen suffering," she stated. "For me, Christ was not to be bought for thirty pieces of silver but with my heart's blood. We buy not cheap in this market." Her life of self-sacrifice was honored well before her death. In 1967, she visited Rome for the last time and, with one other American (an astronaut), she was selected to receive communion from Pope Paul VI. In 1971, she received the *Pacem in Terris* award, named for Pope John XXIII's peace encyclical.

The acclaimed Jesuit publication *America* honored Dorothy Day with a special issue, hailing her as the best exemplar of "the aspiration and action of the American Community during the past forty years." Later, when Day received the *Laetare* medal from Notre Dame University, the presentation drew affectionate laughter—Dorothy was congratulated for "comforting the afflicted and afflicting the comfortable."

By the time of her death on November 29, 1980, Dorothy Day had traveled far from her youthful Bohemian existence. Like Muriel Lester, Day had tried to live out the Gospel, even if that meant unpopular pacifist stands. Like Mother Jones, Day had stood in solidarity with the working poor. Like Birgitta of Sweden, Day was tireless in her religious devotion.

Throughout her adult life, Day seemed to reach back to her early glimpses of Catholicism. As a young journalist in Chicago, she roomed with three other women who were committed to daily prayer and daily Mass. This had made a deep impression on Dorothy.

Although she did not act on this impression for years, Dorothy thought then that "worship, adoration, thanksgiving, supplication..."

are the noblest acts of which we are capable in this life." Even before that experience, as a young girl, Dorothy had came upon a friend's Catholic mother, rapt in private prayer. "I felt a burst of love toward [her] that I have never forgotten," Dorothy later wrote.

Dorothy also remembered where this incident had occurred: in a tenement on Chicago's South Side. Her father had lost his job and the family's life had changed. From life in that tenement, Day had a special understanding of poverty's shame and religion's consolation.

"Whatever I had read as a child about the saints had thrilled me," she recalled. "I could see the nobility of giving one's life for the sick, the maimed, the leper....But there was another question in my mind. Why was so much done to remedy the evil instead of avoiding it in the first place?....Where were the saints to try to change the social order, not just to minister to the slaves, but to do away with slavery?" Dorothy Day's life still challenges us with that question. Where were the saints to try to try to change the social order? Despite her own dismissal of herself as a saint, Day's canonization process has begun.

....

Questions for Reflection and Discussion

1. How would you define Dorothy Day's legacy?
2. What sustained her more than anything?
3. Was she motivated by faith—or arrogance?
4. How does Dorothy Day compare with Mother Teresa of Calcutta?
5. Was Dorothy Day's "mission" egocentric or heroic?
6. How do you reconcile her social radicalism and her religious conservatism?
7. What are Dorothy Day's lessons for our time?
8. Do we need Dorothy Day's kind of commitment today?
9. Could you give fifty-five years for a cause?
10. Where is "the moment of truth" for this heroine?

Ita Ford of El Salvador
(1940-1980)

"All I can share with you is God's palpable presence has never been more real ever since we came to Salvador. He's made a lot of things clear to us...," Ita Ford wrote her mother on September 7, 1980. When people received her letters they always remembered Ita smiling. She still had friends at Sadlier Text Books, where she had worked until 1971. Only nine years ago, people would say later. Only nine years.

Ford became a trusted editor at Sadlier, where she eventually worked on religious texts. She went to parties, enjoyed dancing, and moved from her parents' house in Brooklyn to her own apartment near Greenwich Village. As she traveled with her friend, Kathy Monahan, Ita kept all her father's letters. They were found with her few possessions shortly after her death as a martyred nun in South America.

To look at Ita Ford, no one could guess that she had entered a Maryknoll Missionary convent at the age of twenty-one. Before she could make her final vows, her novice mistress had gently encouraged Ita to leave. The stress had been too much for Ita. "My stomach has been 'on the skity,'" she wrote to a friend. She did not seem physically or emotionally strong enough to be a Maryknoll sister.

Two months later, she wrote again. "I'm home—Wednesday afternoon it was official that I couldn't take vows. It's a shock and a disappointment...but I'll bounce back soon." Ita did not talk about this turn of events to her friends at Sadlier. Even so, she thought about the missionary sisters and kept up an active correspondence with the "Maryknollers" she had known. On an emotional level, her biographer believes, Ita never really left the Order—and she never doubted her faith.

Ten years after Ita Ford had entered Maryknoll, she felt called to try her vocation again. After several applications, she appeared in her boss's doorway. "I'm leaving," she blurted out. "Maryknoll finally accepted me." This time she was sure. Her stomach was not "on the skity." Her vocation had been Ita's greatest dream. Now she was mature enough to handle this stressful calling. Maryknoll sent its sisters to the very poor in very troubled countries.

There were military dictatorships active in South America; there were also Communist insurgents. The government had declared war on the Catholic Church. None of this stopped the Maryknollers.

Before Ita could wonder where she would be sent, however, she had to get through the training that had overwhelmed her before. She came through without any difficulties this time. After her training and her final profession, Ita Ford was sent to Bolivia for language studies and then on to her first mission, near Santiago, Chile. She traveled the tense and troubled country where Maryknollers were active. "Some people say I couldn't have come at a more exciting time while others say this is a terrible introduction," she wrote. "I guess this is indicative of what's going on."

As Ita came to know the Chilean people and their poverty, she felt her presence there was confirmed. She had defied her own experience with failure and self-doubt; she had defied Maryknoll's initial impression of her—and in Chile, it all made sense. Now Ita was defying poverty and injustice themselves for the sake of the Gospel.

Her conscience had led her to the right place for her, at the right time. This set her in a shantytown near Santiago, where Ita lived with other Maryknollers. Her first station was Poblacion Manuel Rodriguez, followed by Poblacion La Bandera. She settled in and quickly adjusted to a radically altered lifestyle. "Home is a small wooden house with three bedrooms and a living-dining-kitchen.... What we hope to be doing here is building community among ourselves, and establishing relationships with some of the people.

"Just what form that will take for me, I still don't know..." she wrote to friends in the States. She had a hand in creating her own ministry. "We are privileged...to know and feel a little of the suffering, of the powerless, those without a voice," Ita wrote.

Sometimes that involved strolling around the square and greeting a man, a woman, perhaps a child. The Maryknollers staffed a women's mental health clinic and Ita worked there as well. What touched her was the pain she saw there, bred by the instability of a country caught in civil war.

"I see Chile deeply experiencing the paschal mystery with the light of Easter still to come...," she reflected. "The cup cannot pass without our drinking it." Ita Ford's vocation in Chile was becoming clearer. "The saving mission of the poor is becoming visible to the Church and offering hope to our world," she wrote.

"Being with the poor," Ita Ford wrote, "means overcoming our distaste for getting dirty literally and metaphorically; the literal dirt, mud, excrement; caring for and supporting the sinner, the underdog, and unpopular causes; entering into messed-up lives; running the risk of being misunderstood, misinterpreted, of being accused as subversives...."

Ita helped widows cope with loss; she provided transportation, helped distribute milk rations, and above all, she listened to those who were overwhelmed by the instability of everyday life. Her own previous struggle with self doubt must have helped her minister to the hopeless people she encountered everywhere.

The nuns were seen as subversives, she knew. Still, her faith sustained her even as the situation became more dangerous. At this point, Ita Ford reached the defining moment of her life. After a required year of reflection, she might have felt called to a less dangerous vocation. Instead, she felt drawn to a country even more troubled than Chile. This was the seething, teeming country of El Salvador.

Here is a deliberate and decisive decision point for Ita Ford. She enters "the pressure cooker" of El Salvador knowing very well that she is putting herself in harm's way—and putting herself at risk for her beliefs. We see how her years in Chile have prepared her for this, her toughest choice. We can see the faith-based motivation that undergirds this determinative move. Through the Mass itself, the words of Jesus have spoken to Ita Ford personally and directly: "This is my body, given for you." Clearly, now, Ita Ford feels called to let these words shape her own life; she will model them. Now , there is no turning back for her. There is only *"adelante"* ("forward")! Ita Ford entered El Salvador as a violent civil war swept the country.

Building for years, the conflict was set off by the government's 1980 assassination of Archbishop Oscar Romero, gunned down at the altar, while he said Mass. The National Guard sent out "death squads" to eliminate all opposition, especially from the poor and the clergy who supported their stand for civil rights.

Ita was fully aware that she had entered a dangerous situation. The poor of El Salvador were bereft without their spiritual leader, someone who had cared deeply for their plight. The Archbishop's murder further destabilized the country. "My timing couldn't be worse, I know," Ita wrote to friends. "...However, once getting here and having the chance to meet and talk with a number of people, I feel differently. It's a privilege to come to a Church of martyrs and people with a strong, committed faith. Though I'm here only two and a half weeks, I have a very strong conviction that I'm where I'm supposed to be...."

Partnered with another Maryknoll sister, Carla Piette, Ita settled into the city of Chalatenango. About two hours from San Salvador, Chalatenango was a busy and productive market town. There the two sisters became workers for an emergency committee sponsored by the church. They dispensed medicines and food, in addition to helping at refugee centers, where many needs were addressed.

Ita understood the political situation all too well. There is nothing naive about Ita's assessment of the turmoil in the country. She noted that it was complicated by the differing ideals of the rebel groups and the generalized panic caused by the unchecked army activity. Every night, the sisters heard gunfire. The army was fighting a variety of populist groups that wanted a new government. "I don't think we could have dreamed this job up before we came,"

Ita observed in her journal, writing on while machine guns rattled in the darkness beyond.

Ita and Carla needed a way to help the poor in the hills beyond the city. Somehow they managed to acquire a second-hand jeep. This vehicle was helpful during the rainy season—until Ita and Carla went to rescue a young man who was accused of supporting guerrillas. While the sisters crossed the El Chapote River, the jeep overturned. Carla pushed her friend out and Ita floated two miles down river. She managed to survive this sudden accident, but when she returned to Chalatenango, Ita learned that Carla had drowned. Ita selected the readings for the funeral and "stayed strong" for Carla's memory.

Back in the United States, the Ford family became increasingly concerned about Ita's safety. "I know this is a very hard time for you," Ita wrote to her mother. "I know that you're concerned and worried about the situation and I don't know how to alleviate that. I truly believe that I should be here...."

In her private reflections, however, Ita notes that there are sometimes forty to fifty, to a hundred assassinations a day in El Salvador. Even so, in nine months "there were twenty-eight assassinations of Church personnel...and thirty-three seizures of Church properties," Ita told the Maryknoll Assembly in Nicaragua on November 24, 1980.

Thanksgiving was celebrated there, and on December 2, Ita flew back to El Salvador with Sister Maura Clarke. They were not deterred from their sense of calling. Ita's last letter to her mother was positive: "I guess we're into celebrating life—birth, birthdays, and my own acknowledgment that I'm still alive....So here's to three generations of Fords thankful for the gift of life!"

Upon their return, Ita and Maura were greeted at the airport by Sister Dorothy Kazel (an Ursuline sister), and lay assistant Jean

Donovan. They piled into the sisters' recognizable white van and headed back toward their base. They could not know that they were awaited by five armed men, members of the National Guard led by Sergeant Colindres Aleman. They had been watching the sisters. Now the guardsmen would carry out their orders. Thirty minutes down the road, they stopped the van. Three guardsmen entered it and drove it toward the National Guard command post at El Rosario la Paz. In the van, there was silence. The women must have realized that they were facing their final hour.

Another National Guardsman got into the van and drove it down rutted back roads to a cow pasture outside San Pedro Nonualco. The women were ordered to get out of the van and wait in the pasture. That was where a farmer, Gomez Alfaro, found them early the next morning when he went to milk his cows. Several yards from his house, he saw the stripped bodies of four women. By ten o'clock, when Alfaro returned, he saw that the bodies had been buried in a shallow mass grave.

Notified by the villagers, a justice of the peace had ordered this action. The women were referred to as "unknowns." Two days later, Alfaro learned that the three of these "unknowns" had been American nuns. By December 4, the local parish priest was notified. He, in turn, contacted the vicar of the San Vicente diocese, and the American Embassy was informed.

By the afternoon of December 4, United States Ambassador Robert White had arrived on the scene. With permission of the local Justice of the Peace, White ordered the opening of the shallow grave in the cow pasture. There were the bodies of the four women, stacked on top of each other. The first exhumed body was Jean Donovan's. The last was Ita Ford's, pulled up from the bottom of the pit. The women had been beaten, raped, and shot to death. The killing was "execution style": A bullet in the back of each head. The Maryknoll sisters, Ita Ford and Maura Clarke, had left final instructions, which were carried out. They were buried with the poor in El Salvador, where their graves are marked with simple white crosses.

The families of the victims fought a long battle for justice, which did not come for several years. The immediate response from United Nations Ambassador-Designate Jeane Kirkpatrick declared that the women were not just nuns—they were "gunrunners." This outrageous statement prompted a great outcry from the Catholic Church in America and around the world.

Even so, it was not until 1983 that the shooters were convicted of homicide. Finally, in 1993, the United Nations Truth Commission gave an accurate report of the identity of the churchwomen and an account of their final hours. The orders of their murderers were also exposed.

But that was not the last word on Ita Ford. The week before her murder, Ita's niece received a birthday letter from her aunt. "This is a terrible time in El Salvador for youth," Ita had written. "A lot of idealism and commitment are getting snuffed out here now. The reasons why so many people are being killed are quite complicated, but there are some clear, simple strands. One is that people have found a meaning to live, to sacrifice, struggle, and even die. And whether their life spans sixteen years, sixty or ninety, for them, their lives had a purpose. In many ways, they are fortunate people."

The letter continues with words that defy the last scene in that rural cow-pasture. "Brooklyn is not passing through the drama of El Salvador," Ita went on. "But some things hold true wherever one is, and at whatever age. What I'm saying is that I hope you can come to find that which gives life a deep meaning for you, something that energizes you, enthuses you, enables you to keep moving ahead."

This is a message left for many of us, as well. Ita Ford's forty years show us how crucial it is to discover one's vocation and live it out, whatever the cost. Whether people's lives "span sixteen years, sixty, or ninety," Ita Ford's words still echo, "for them, their lives had a purpose."

···

Questions for Reflection and Discussion

1. How would you define Ita Ford's example?
2. What sustained her more than anything?
3. Was she out to prove herself—or do you think she had a genuine calling?
4. Why do you think Ita Ford stayed in El Salvador's war zone?
5. What was Ford's "mission" in South America?
6. Do you think Ford was selfish regarding the family she left behind?
7. What can Ford's life teach us in our time?
8. Do we need Ford's kind of commitment today?
9. Would you work in a country as dangerous as El Salvador was?
10. Where is "the moment of truth" for this heroine?

Mothers of the Disappeared
(Late 1970s-1983)

The women were silent. Dressed in black, they moved together. On their heads they wore white scarves. In their hands were photographs of their lost children. In the midst of Buenos Aires, a public square enclosed them. The Plaza de Mayo took on a different aura when these *Madres* were present.

They faced the building that housed Argentina's Ministry of the Interior. They also faced the possibility of arrest, detention, or worse. The ruling military *junta* had strictly outlawed public protests of any kind, anywhere. Still the women gathered together. Still they moved in somber silence. For some time, they were not disturbed. At the central plaza, they arrived at three-thirty in the afternoon every Thursday. Was that day of the week specially selected or was it simply convenient? During Holy Week, the Last Supper is always commemorated on a Thursday, as is another event: Christ's agony at Gethsemane. These women, too, shared a heartfelt agony. It was evident on their faces and their dress. This was no upbeat rally. This, quite clearly, was a stately vigil.

Drawn together by tragedy, the *Madres* had all lost grown children to Argentina's new dictatorship, installed by a recent *coup d'etat*. For the next seven years or so, the government's security forces targeted citizens deemed "unpatriotic," from students to activists, union members to university faculty. This suppression of freedom was carried out insidiously, almost invisibly. For years, no one knew precisely how it was carried out. Years passed before the details came to light and the truth was known.

Meanwhile, unlike other military *juntas*, this one would seek to maintain a certain pretense. The pretense was this: the country was undisturbed, unchanged. There would be no gruesome corpses left in ditches. There would be no machine guns firing on crowds. The government would create a semblance of order, calm, normality. At this, it succeeded—on the surface.

Beneath the surface there lay a different scene. So-called "subversives" were swiftly and silently abducted, often from their beds at midnight. In hidden camps, they were detained, tortured, murdered. Their bodies were never found. They became known as the *desaparecidos*: "The Disappeared." Eventually, their numbers reached thirty thousand. No organization or individual dared speak out on their behalf—not the national press, not the church, nor officials, nor local politicians. There was only one sign of reminder, of rebellion. Only the *"Madres de Plaza de Mayo"* dared to embody their rage and remembrance. The women's presence was consistent, quiet, and courageous. It spoke eloquently in silence. Its visibility grew and eventually, it could not be ignored. In the beginning, however, the women's influence seemed unlikely, at best.

The Mothers had encountered one another in offices, prisons, hospitals, courts—anywhere they hoped to discover information about their missing children. Instead, the Mothers had discovered a sense of solidarity with others like themselves: those who remained. The women prayed together in churches and passed surreptitious notes indicating the location of the next meetings. They wept together, they grieved together. This common support was crucial. It led to the next stage: Turning grief into action.

Here lies the watershed moment for the Mothers of the Disappeared. Together, this group of women took their sorrow to another level; the level of action. Motivated by deep religious faith and a strong sense of solidarity, the *Madres* manifested mourning in a new way: their visible, silent, steady presence, offered in lasting protest. When these "defiant daughters" entered the Plaza de Mayo, they went against all expectations of female behavior—and indeed, behavior under the ruling *junta*. The Mothers' decision to do so was to be an enduring one.

"The decision to install a permanent weekly presence in Plaza de Mayo was an act of desperation, rather than one of calculated political resistance," writes Jo Fisher, a chronicler of the movement. "It was a sense of desperation which the women believed only other mothers who had lost children would share." Two things sustained them: their faith—and their sisterhood. They would join these

The white shawl of the Mothers, painted on the ground in Plaza de Mayo, Buenos Aires

with their bereavement and let it fuel them to protest the plight of the *Desaparecidos*. In the beginning, there was no example to follow, no blueprint, no organized plan, says the book *Mothers of the Disappeared*. At first, the Mothers walked in pairs around the edges of the square.

If they stopped moving, police would point rifles at them and command them to move on. Defiant and undismayed, the women decided they were not noticeable enough. They wanted to present a strong visible presence.

And so, as a group, they began to move slowly around the square's central monument. They were noticed but not supported. Even close sympathizers dared not draw near. "It was very dangerous for them to approach us," said María del Rosario. "We were very alone in the beginning."

The police were baffled. They did not know how to handle these women. After all, this government had elevated motherhood and family values to the highest degree. What could be done to a group of middle-aged mothers who walked silently in the public square? The first solution seemed to take the form of ridicule and dismissal. The *Madres* were brushed off with denigrating insults. "*Las locas de Plaza de Mayo*," they were called. "Crazy women." The government tried to portray the Mothers as laughable. This attitude, in turn, seemed laughable. It was obvious: One look at the women's demeanor, dress, and photographs told the real story.

Still, this form of retribution was mild. It could have been worse —and soon it was. The Mothers received spiritual support from a French nun, Alicia Doman, who ministered for twenty years in Argentina. Sister Alicia became a kind of unofficial chaplain to the group. She had been sent by the Toulouse Institute of the Sisters of the Foreign Mission. By 1977, Alicia Doman was deeply immersed in the cause of the Mothers. While designing a Christmas retreat for them, she was abducted as she returned from a meeting. No one saw her or heard from her again. Sister Alicia had fallen into that dreaded category. She had become one of the *Desaparecidos*.

While the Mothers grieved for their friend and comforter, they began to receive menacing calls and letters. Occasionally, without warning, they were seized and detained by the police for twenty-four hours. They were always released, unharmed.

The Mothers did not fear these increasingly aggressive moves. One of them wrote, "When a mother loses a child, that pain is stronger than fear or terror." The women's story began leaking out to the foreign press. Now they could not be harassed without publicity. They could, however, be barred from the square. For much of 1979, the Plaza de Mayo was sealed off and filled with police. The *Madres* were confined to its edges. The protestors stood firm. "When a woman gives birth to a child, she lives life and at the same time, when they cut the cord, she gives freedom," one of the

Mothers stated. "We were fighting for life and for freedom. It was our insistence, our refusal to give up, that made us effective."

In their black dresses, holding their photos and their rosaries, the mute women comprised the only visible group defying the widespread reign of terror. Somehow their story penetrated Argentina's news ban and the vigil-keepers captured the national imagination. It was as if this group, taken together, embodied the very word "conscience" itself.

Fighting back, the Mothers legitimized their organization by registering it legally. With this registration came an important written declaration of who they were and what they would do. The statement ended with ringing words: "Finally, we believe in an Argentina where there is justice, where the law is respected, and where it is possible to live in liberty, tolerance, and respect."

The document was printed, published, and publicized. It was also circulated among the foreign press. Offshoots of the group sprang up in the towns of Mendoza and La Plata. The Buenos Aires group met at Mendoza during that difficult year of 1979.

"By then we had a very clear idea of what the struggle was about," said Elsa de Becerra. "That it wasn't just for one child, but for all the *Desaparecidos*. We began to march every Thursday in the main square here in Mendoza with our white head scarves...at midday, the time when the most people were around. When we could, we went to Buenos Aires.

"Plaza de Mayo is the center of our struggle. For us it's like a meeting place with our disappeared children." With them were women who were also searching for their grandchildren. There were many others in that position.

The *Abuelas* (grandmas) *de Plaza de Mayo* met at bus stops and cafés and eventually found foreign support. "At the end of 1979," said María del Rosario, "we decided that even if they took us prisoner, even if they killed us, we would return to the square (Plaza de Mayo) on the first Thursday of the new year. The first time the police didn't react. We'd taken them by surprise. The second week they were waiting. They detained a lot of us but they had to let us go because we were already well-known abroad....The beatings and threats continued but that year we returned to the square and they were never able to stop us again. They pulled our hair, they stopped buses and dragged us inside, but the next Thursday we were back again. We brought foreign journalists so they could see what was happening."

Aida de Suárez explained how important it was for the Mothers to be back at Plaza de Mayo. "We never stopped our marches. In some way we were always there. If there were twenty of us, there were twenty. If there were fifty, there were fifty....On Thursdays at half past three, this square belongs to us."

The women had grown stronger and more outspoken. The president of the Association of the Mothers of the Disappeared, Hebe de Bonafini declared: "We have thirty thousand *desaparecidos* today because the leadership of the Church and the unions, as much as the political leadership, allowed it."

In 1981, the Mothers instigated the *Marcha de Resistencia* (March of Resistance). They marched in the square for twenty-four consecutive hours in protest against the dictators. A second march was planned for December 1982. Just before it could occur, a telegram arrived at the association's headquarters, The Mothers House. All were summoned to the police station and reminded that their actions were illegal. The women refused to sign any statements, but the march was canceled by the government.

The police surrounded Plaza de Mayo and barred anyone from entering it. The women were not stymied. They marched down the Avenue de Mayo, a major thoroughfare leading to the square.

Thousands of people joined that march. Cafés and shops put chairs out on the sidewalks for the women. "There was a great feeling of solidarity," said Elisa de Landin, "in spite of the fact that we still had the military in power....It was a very emotional demonstration for us because it showed that people were ready to take a stand against the military government."

Perhaps it was prayer and publicity that saved the women from drastic consequences. Sporadically, after seizure and detention, the Mothers must have wondered if this time they, too, would join the thousands of the "Disappeared." But the vigil of these so-called "crazy women" could not be crushed by conventional means. If this cadre of devoted mothers abruptly vanished, the world's conscience would be aroused. An international incident might occur. Valuable foreign support could be lost.

The unthinkable had happened: Some fifty faithful women, lacking experience or political power, had checkmated an entire military *junta*, its police and its security forces, and sparked the transformation of their country.

Carmen de Guede recalls "one time when we went to the square and the police had it blocked off with metal barriers, and men with

Poster of the Disappeared, November 2005

rifles and grenades were trying to push us back....We stood on the (cathedral's) steps with our banner, *'Queremos a nuestros hijos'* (We want our children)."

Every time the women tried to get back into the plaza the police chased them out with weapons drawn. "We began to sing the national anthem, and I don't know why but when they hear the national anthem, the police and the army have to lower their weapons. When we finished it we began to sing it again and again so they couldn't raise their guns...."

Throughout their ordeal, the women stayed true to their consciences. With extraordinary endurance, they kept up their vigil, their nonviolent protests, and their stance for several years. "When everyone was terrorized we didn't stay at home crying," said one of the Mothers. "We went to the streets to confront them (the government) directly. We were mad, but it was the only way to stay sane."

The aftermath of grief, of course, would always linger. But the Mothers were uniquely equipped to understand and console one another. When the Church failed them, these women became their own church, praying for the group and for its lost ones.

"Las Madres de Plaza de Mayo" outlasted the military *junta* that had stolen their children. In 1983, the government was forced to surrender its power to civilian rule.

The discredited *junta* finally admitted that there had indeed been *Desaparecidos*. Later that year, disturbing revelations began to surface: thirty-three concentration camps in Tucumán; long detentions; torture before the "Disappeared" were murdered. Many were buried in secret locations. Some were pushed out of airplanes over the sea. In 1995, a pilot on these "death flights" confirmed this.

There would be no reunions, except for some of the grandmothers, who searched diligently for their children's children. Still, the Mothers had come a long way since 1977. When the group had formed, "we each put the name of our own child on the head scarves," said María del Rosario.

"And then we changed it to all the *Desaparecidos*, because now we aren't fighting for just one but for all of them....For us there is only one future, to continue the struggle until the day we die, so that justice will be the guarantee of life in the Republic of Argentina."

During the Mothers' vigil, there was an unrelated terrorist incident which destroyed the town of El Mozete in El Salvador. Perhaps the memorial in that town's plaza speaks to "The *Madres*" as well. The memorial's inscription expresses the resurrection faith that sustains them. Referring to all who were lost, the inscription reads: "They did not die, they are with us, with you, and with all humanity."

....

Questions for Reflection and Discussion

1. How would you explain the Mothers' mission?
2. What sustained them more than anything?
3. Were they motivated by faith—or anger? Could they have been motivated by both?
4. Did their courage put them at risk? Were they willing to pay the price?
5. Was the Mothers' "mission" idealistic or heroic or both?
6. Do you think they were "driven" or "called?" Could they have been both?
7. Do you think the Mothers were right to follow a "higher law?"
8. Where do we need the Mothers' kind of commitment today?
9. Would you engage in nonviolent protests for the sake of justice?
10. Where is "the moment of truth" for these heroines?

EPILOGUE
Immaculée Ilibagiza of Rwanda
(1972-)

She would not give in. She would not cry out. She would not let the killers win. Ultimately, she would defy them with her fortitude and her faith. Crouched in hiding, she could hear the death squad on the other side of the wall. With machetes and spears, they searched the house.

They had murdered thousands and they would not hesitate to murder her. Suddenly, she heard them calling her name: "Find her— find Immaculée." Gripping her rosary, she held her breath and prayed in silence: "You tell us in the Bible that if we ask, we shall receive... well, God, I am asking." At last the men's footsteps retreated. They banged out of the house but they would be back—again and again. That was a certainty. It was the spring of 1994. Civil war had just broken out in Rwanda.

When its president's plane was shot down, the Hutu tribe turned on its Tutsi tribal neighbors. There had long been tensions and conflicts between the two ethnic groups. Tutsis were members of a more educated, wealthy minority—and now Hutu extremists had targeted them for genocide.

Now, in central Africa, Rwanda's beautiful green and rolling land literally ran with blood. The killing fields were everywhere, from streets to homes to a stadium.

Within three months, nearly one million Tutsi children, women, and men were murdered, many of them hacked to death by machetes. Most of Immaculée's family was among them, though she did not discover the scope of the tragedy until she had emerged from hiding. For ninety-one days, she huddled with seven other women in a secret refuge: the tiny spare bathroom in a neighbor's house.

This neighbor, a moderate Hutu, was a family friend—and a Christian minister whose faith transcended ethnic divisions. Risking his own life, the pastor agreed to shelter Immaculée when her father, sensing trouble, had sought protection for his only daughter. None of them could imagine what lay ahead.

The pastor's spare bathroom was only three feet by four feet; the women had to sit on top of each other, occasionally standing up to shift and stretch. They could not talk; they could not wash. Their food supply was small. At the end of her ninety-one day ordeal,

Immaculée had lost forty pounds, as had her comrades in the shelter. And yet, Immaculée's Catholic faith deepened. It sustained her throughout this time of terror and suffering. To use her own words, she discovered God amidst the Rwandan holocaust.

"All I could do was pray," Immaculée wrote later. "So that's what I did....I came to learn that God never shows us something we aren't ready to understand. Instead, he lets us see what we need to see, when we need to see it. He'll wait until our eyes and hearts are open to him, and then when we're ready, he will plant our feet on the path that's best for us...but it's up to us to do the walking."

Eventually, she literally did just that. Her faith gave her strength. "I believe God spared my life," she later wrote. Physically restricted, Immaculée used her mind. Once a student at the prestigious *Lycee de L'Afrique,* she decided to teach herself English. At her request, Immaculée's host offered her a French-English dictionary and two English books. "I took a deep breath and thanked God for answering my prayers...," she later wrote. Soon she would be able to read the Bible in a new language.

"Even though I'd be losing prayer time, I knew that God would be with me while I studied. He intended for me to learn this language, and I could feel the power of his intention coursing through me. I could not waste a minute of my time in self-pity or doubt. God had presented me with a gift, and my gift in return would be to make the most of his kindness."

Immaculée persisted in her studies, even after the death squad again searched the pastor's house. Her spirit "tumbled backwards into the arms of fear and doubt. Her throat closed; she could not swallow. Feeling faint, she finally lost consciousness. In a dream-state, she "floated like a feather above the other women." This mystical experience remained indelibly in her memory. "I saw them (the women) trembling below me on the floor, holding their Bibles on their heads, begging God for mercy," Immaculée went on. "I looked up and saw Jesus hovering above me in a pool of golden light, and his arms were reaching toward me," she reported. Her body's aches and pains disappeared. The spiritual support sustained her.

She could hear the killers singing as they walked away from the house. That night, however, the pastor brought bad news. He had fired one of his servants who was now angry—and suspicious. Another kept asking to clean the spare bathroom; he, too, seemed suspicious. In the pastor's opinion his house was no longer a safe hiding place. Almost immediately, events proved him to be right.

During the next week, the killers returned and tore the pastor's bedroom apart. Frustrated, they swore to come back the next day—and this time, they would find the hidden Tutsi women. In desperation, the pastor had managed to contact a garrison of French soldiers; they had just camped nearby. Immaculée urged him to let the women go that night and run for their lives to the French camp.

At two in the morning, for the first time in three months, the women left the bathroom and stepped outside. For a moment, they took deep breaths of the fresh night air. Then, under cover of darkness, they would move quickly toward a small camp of French soldiers. The women, weakened by their ordeal, gathered their strength and walked a long way to reach the French. When they arrived, however, the fugitives' exhilaration was short-lived. The French troops moved on and abandoned the women.

Summoning her courage, Immaculée led the women through dangerous territory to an outpost of rebel Tutsis, who took them in. Soon after this escape, the horror abated beyond them. After the fall of Kigali, Rwanda's capital city, the genocidal fervor died down. Now, however, the women had to confront the horrifying aftermath of their country's holocaust. Out of every four Tutsis, three were dead. Children had been cut down in cold blood. Many victims had been drastically mutilated before they were killed. One of these was Immaculée's brother. Another brother had been herded into a sports stadium with thousands of others; everyone there was murdered. Then the stadium, with its corpses, had been set on fire. The emotional shocks kept coming to Immaculée and her companions. Her father, a prosperous teacher, had been shot while he brought food to a neighbor's children. Mr. Ilibagiza's body was then used as a roadblock. His wife, also a teacher, had been hacked to death. In anguish and in tears, Immaculée was faced with her life's greatest challenge. Only twenty-two, she had to undertake a task for which there was no preparation: recovering the remains of her closest relatives.

Once this was accomplished, she had her family buried near the site of the burnt-out family home. In her diary, and in a filmed report, Immaculée laid her head against her house and wept bitterly. Her next challenge was the hardest: the inner struggle against bitterness, rage, and grief.

At a friend's house, Immaculée collapsed outside and lay on the ground, looking up at the stars. "I cried until I had no more tears," she wrote. "I thought about what Jesus had promised me in my dream and I began talking to him....Everything I loved in this world has been taken away. I'm putting my life in your hands, Jesus...keep your promise and take care of me. I will keep my promise—I will be your faithful daughter. I closed my eyes and pictured the faces of my family, and I prayed that God would keep them close and warm." For some time, Immaculée lived at a large, guarded French fort.

The troops had arranged armored vehicles in a semi-circle to protect the Tutsis who fled there. "The French said their job was to protect us, and they did it well," Immaculée wrote in her diary. "I never once felt threatened by the killers while I was at the camp. However, Hutus did often gather along the outer perimeter, peering

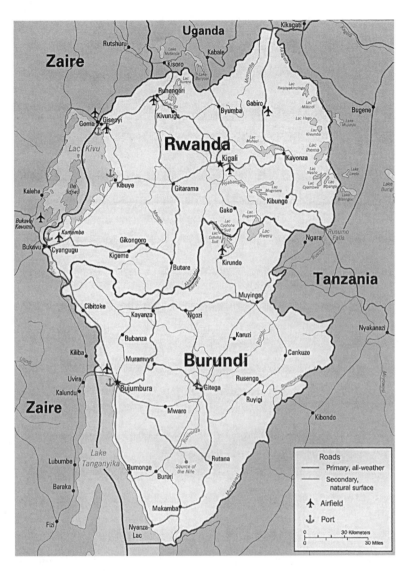

between the armored cars to catch a glimpse of us. They stared at us like zoo animals...sole survivors of a species hunted to the brink of extinction." When the French pulled out of Rwanda, Immaculée was sheltered by Tutsi forces in a Baptist church. There were no beds or blankets, but Immaculée writes that it felt good to her to be in a house of God. Other Tutsi survivors stayed there as well, but this was a temporary shelter.

Immaculée knew she would have to leave Rwanda. In the damaged city of Kigali, she made her way to United Nations headquarters. Now, she realized, God had directed her to learn English. Knowledge of that language enabled Immaculée to obtain a job at the UN.

This job overwhelmed Immaculée with gratitude, and she began to work with Rwandan orphans—like herself. Even as her life stabilized and the Rwandan situation improved, Immaculée was still tormented. She yearned for revenge on her family's killers. "I felt the bitter, dirty taste of hatred in my mouth," she wrote. Inwardly, she raged at the murderers: "Those bloody animals! They are animals, animals, animals!" But her conscience would not leave her alone with these thoughts.

Immaculée knew she was turning away from God and the teachings of Jesus. One night, unable to sleep, she left her bed to pray on her knees. "Take this pain from me and cleanse my heart," she implored God. "Fill me with the power of your love and forgiveness. Those who did these horrible things are still your children...help me to forgive them. Oh God, help me to love them."

Driven by her conscience and her faith, Immaculée went on an unexpected journey. She gained permission to visit her family's murderers in prison. There she saw Felicien, once a killer with the death squad that had hunted her. Now Immaculée was able to view him in a radically different way. She said she saw how evil had poisoned him, eating him away. And now he stood before her, weeping.

Immaculée put out her hand to him. "I forgive you," she said. Felicien wept harder. "I forgive you," she said again. "How could you do that?" the guard demanded. "Forgiveness is all I have to offer," said Immaculée Ilibagiza. Again, driven by conscience, courage, and faith, she had defied the power of hatred itself.

"God saved my soul and spared my life for a reason," Immaculée wrote in her autobiographical book, *Left to Tell: Finding God Amidst the Rwandan Holocaust*. "He left me to tell my story to others and show as many people as possible the healing power of his love and forgiveness.

"There are people I left behind that I must help. I hope to return to Rwanda as often as I can to aid in restoring hope to the hearts of genocide survivors, especially orphaned children. I am currently setting up a foundation that will help victims of genocide and war everywhere to heal in body, mind, and spirit. God's message extends beyond borders...."

Several years after the Rwandan genocide, Immaculée returned to her native country, where she sought out others who had murdered her family. To them, she also offered her forgiveness. Anger, she had discovered, only prolonged her pain. Christ's command to love one's enemies was one she wanted to live out. "The love of a single heart can make a world of difference. I believe that we can heal Rwanda—and our world—by healing one heart at a time." Now a woman on a mission, Immaculée did not revisit her home alone. Her husband, Bryan, accompanied her, with their young son.

Immaculée's life has moved on, though she will always carry the scars of the genocide with her. A resident of New York City, she still works at the United Nations. She has started a fund for Rwandan orphans and written three books about her experiences, hoping her words will help others.

Immaculée's defiance of the darkness speaks powerfully to us. Her response to daunting challenges was rooted in constant prayer. Immaculée's triumphs show us our great need for inspiring figures such as hers. She stands in a long line of heroines, often overlooked, whose lives reach across the centuries and connect with her own. Rooted in a strong tradition, women of conscience stand behind her, casting their light ahead of their times, into our futures and those of our children.

....

Questions for Reflection and Discussion

1. How would you define Immaculée's example?
2. What sustained her more than anything?
3. Was she motivated by faith—or terror? Could she have been motivated by both?
4. How did she support the pastor who hid her?
5. Why was Immaculée's defiance of terror supported by her faith?
6. Do you think Immaculée would have given herself away without her faith?
7. What can Immaculée's life teach us today?
8. How was Immaculée able to forgive?
9. Could you forgive your family's murderers?
10. Where is "the moment of truth" for this heroine?

Author's Note

This is a book I have wanted to write since my childhood. I was raised on stories of heroines and heroes who fought battles of conscience. I also spent hours reading about spiritual heroines in such varied contexts as *Landmark Books* and Butler's *Lives of the Saints*. Throughout my life, I have been fascinated by spiritual women in principled dilemmas. As an adult, I have written historical novels about Harriet Tubman, Anne Hutchinson, Mother Seton and Mother Jones. It is an honor and a joy to profile the women who appear on the pages of *Defiant Daughters*.

As noted in the introduction, it was inevitable that some spiritual heroines could not be included in this volume. It is encouraging to note the great number of "defiant daughters" in history, although many have been overlooked or discounted. This book's focus on the Christian tradition does not in any way deny the presence of principled spiritual women in other traditions.

Also as noted in the introduction, I have tried to find the center of each story in terms of dilemmas and decision points. It seems to me that deeply felt faith has been the common denominator here. Faith challenged these women in various ways. Some have been mystics; some have felt drawn to alleviate suffering; others have felt the need to stand in solidarity with the poor. Many have been strongly motivated by the Gospel passage in Matthew 25 in which Jesus states, "Whatever you did for one of these least brothers of mine, you did for me."

As an historical novelist, I am experienced with the interstices that exist in historical portraits. Each of the profiles here are sourced and grounded in fact. In some cases, I have drawn deductions and informed assumptions from the historical sources. I have indicated areas where I have made such deductions, assumptions, and conjectures.

This book attempts to integrate defiance with spiritual grounding. My criteria for these profiles have been a combination of spirituality, defiance and conscientious dilemmas. It is notable that, in all cases, the choices are costly and always involve serious sacrifice.

This is true among women from different countries, cultures, and eras. The purpose of the book is to provide inspiring role models, to be sure, but also to examine what the great theologian Dietrich Bonhoeffer has called "The Cost of Discipleship." That cost, he knew, would always be present.

In the 1960s, the noted playwright Robert Bolt wrote an instant classic, *A Man for All Seasons*, about the spiritual dilemma of Saint Thomas More. I was fortunate to see this play as a girl, and it made a lasting impression on me. It also left me with a desire to learn more about "Women for All Seasons" of More's ilk. It is high time for such a gallery and it is an honor to reflect on one here. These lives not only lift our sights and evoke our admiration, they also challenge our own values and levels of commitment to our beliefs. This is not always a comfortable road—but it presents us with gifted guides.

I offer my gratitude to these guides, as well as to my own "soul sisters" for their affection and support during the writing of this book.

~MH 2010

Sources and
Acknowledgments

Every effort has been made to locate and secure permission from the rights holders of copyrighted material that is quoted in this book. If any such acknowledgments have been inadvertently omitted, the publisher would appreciate receiving full information so that proper credit may be given in any future editions.

The sources cited here are quoted in the book or were consulted by the author in preparing the book.

Adams, Jeremy duQuesnay, translator and revisor. *Joan of Arc: Her Story*. (New York: St. Martin's Griffin, 1998).

American Carpatho-Russian Orthodox Diocese of the U.S.A. *St. Maria Skobstsova of Paris: Martyr of Ravensbrück* (NY: Houghton Mifflin Company, 1990).

Anderson, Maxwell, *Joan of Lorraine* (a play). Copyright © 1946; 1947 by Maxwell Anderson. Copyright renewal © 1974 by Gilda Anderson and children. All rights in and to the play are reserved. Used by permission.

Balasundaram, Franklyn J., editor, *Martyrs in the History of Christianity*, Ch. 5, "The Martyrdom of Marie Skobtsova (1891–1945)" by Chanda Sahi. Copyright © 1999 ISPCK (Indian Society for Promoting Christian Knowledge). All rights reserved. Used by permission of publisher.

Beevers, John. *St. Teresa of Avila* (Garden City, NY: Doubleday, 1961).

Beilin, Elaine V. editor, *The Examinations of Anne Askew: Women Writers 1350–1850*. (NY: Oxford University Press, 1996).

Bielecki, Tessa. *Teresa of Avila: Mystical Writings* (NY: Crossroad, 1994).

Bostridge, Mark. Excerpts from "Pop and Flo," "To Be Happy in My Own Way," "Calamity Unparalleled," and "A Visible March to Heaven" from

Florence Nightingale: The Making of an Icon by Mark Bostridge. Copyright © 2008 by Mark Bostridge. Reprinted by permission of Farrar, Straus and Giroux, LLC.

Bradford, Sarah H. *Scenes From the Life of Harriet Tubman.* (Beaufort, SC: Beaufort Books, 1971).

Bradford, Sarah. *Harriet Tubman, the Moses of Her People.* (Bedford, MA: Applewood Books, 1886).

Brett, Donna Whitson & Edward T. *Murdered in Central America.* (Maryknoll, NY: Orbis Press, 1988).

Brooks, Polly Schoyer. *Beyond The Myth: The Story of Joan of Arc* (New York: Houghton Mifflin Company, 1990).

Brosius, Shirley, editor. *Sisterhood of Faith: 365 Life-Changing Stories About Women Who Made a Difference.* (New York: Howard Books, 2006).

Christian Community of Laura Lopez. *Vida y Testimonio de Laura.* (El Salvador, 1987).

Clinton, Catherine. *Harriet Tubman: The Road to Freedom.* (Boston: Back Bay Books, 2005).

Cruz, Joan Carroll. *Saintly Women of Modern Times.* (Huntingdon, IN: Our Sunday Visitor Press, 1992). Copyright © 2004 by Joan Carroll Cruz. Used by permission of Our Sunday Visitor, 200 Noll Plaza, Huntington, IN, 46750, 1-800-348-2440, www.osv.com. No other use is authorized.

Day, Dorothy. *The Long Loneliness.* (New York: Harper & Row, 1952).

Day, Dorothy. *The Long Loneliness.* (Chicago: Saint Thomas More Press, 1993).

Deen, Edith. *Great Women of the Christian Faith.* (Westwood, NJ: Barbour and Company, 1959).

Dirvin, Joseph I. *The Soul of Elizabeth Seton: A Spiritual Portrait.* (San Francisco: Ignatius Press, 1990).

Dossey, Barbara Montgomery. *Florence Nightingale: Mystic, Visionary, Healer.* (Philadelphia, PA: F.A. Davis Company, 2010).

Dragon, O. Antonio. *Maria de la Luz, Protomartyr of Catholic Action.* (Beaufort, SC: Sands Publishing, 1938).

Dumbach & Jud Newbborn. *Sophia Scholl and the White Rose.* (Oxford, UK: Oneworld Publications, 1986, 2006).

Ellsberg, Robert. *Blessed Among All Women: Women Saints, Prophets, and Witnesses for Our Time.* (New York: Crossroad Publishing Company, 2005).

Evans, Jeanne, editor. *Here I Am, Lord: The Letters and Writings of Ita Ford.* (Maryknoll, NY: Orbis Books, 2005) Copyright © 2005 by Jeanne Evans and the Maryknoll Sisters of St. Dominic, Inc. All rights reserved. Used by permission of Orbis Books.

Fethering, Dale. *The Miners' Angel: A Portrait.* (Carbondale, IL: Southern Illinois U. Press, 1974).

Fisher, Jo. *Mothers of the Disappeared.* (Boston: South End Press, 1989). Copyright © Jo Fisher, 1989. Used by permission of South End Press.

Fitzgerald, Kyriaki Karidoyanes. *Women Deacons in the Orthodox Church: Called to Holiness and Ministry.* (Brookline, MA: Holy Cross Orthodox Press, 1999).

Fitzgerald, Kyriaki Karidoyanes, Ed. *Encountering Women of Faith.* (Berkeley, CA: InterOrthodox Press, 2005).

Forest, Jim. *Love is the Measure: A Biography of Dorothy Day.* (Maryknoll, New York: Orbis Books, 1993).

Forest, Jim. *A Biography of Dorothy Day,* an essay prepared for *The Encyclopedia of American Catholic History* (Collegeville, MN: Liturgical Press, 1997); available at Catholic Worker website [www.catholicworker.com/ddaybio.htm]). All rights reserved. Used by permission of Liturgical Press.

Foxe, John. *Foxe's Book of Martyrs.* (Blacksburg, VA.: Wilder Publications, 2009).

Foxe, John, and John Cumming. *Book of Martyrs and the Acts and Monuments of the Christian Church, Part I.* (London: UK: Kessinger Publishing, 1875).

Glynn, Paul. *The Smile of a Ragpicker* (Hunters Hill, Australia: Marist Fathers Books, 1992). Used by permission of author.

Golden, Renny. *The Hour of the Poor, the Hour of Women: Salvadoran Women Speak.* (New York: Crossroad Publishing Co, 1991). Copyright © 1991 by Renny Golden. All rights reserved. Used by permission of author.

Gorn, Elliot J. *The Most Dangerous Woman in America.* (New York: Farrar, Strauss, Giroux Publishers, 2002).

Hackel, Sergei. *Pearl of Great Price: The Life of Maria Skobtsova.* (Crestwood, NY: St. Vladimir's Seminary Press, 1982). © 1965, Sergei Hackel, © 1982, revised edition, Sergei Hackel. Used by permission of Darton, Longman & Todd, Ltd via Copyright Clearance Center.

Harrison, Eugene Myers. Blazing the Missionary Trail (Chicago: Scripture Press Books, 1949).

Heidish, Marcy. A Woman Called Moses. (Boston: Houghton Mifflin Company, 1976).

Heidish, Marcy. Miracles: A Novel Based on the Life of Elizabeth Seton. (New York: New American Library, 1984).

Heidish, Marcy. Witnesses. (Boston: Houghton Mifflin Company, 1980).

Hollyday, Joyce. 'Ain't I a Woman?' (Sojourners Magazine, December 1986).

Ilibagiza, Immaculée (with Steve Erwin). Led by Faith: Rising From the Ashes of the Rwandan Genocide. (Carlsbad, CA: Hay House, 2008).

Ilibagiza, Immaculée (with Steve Erwin). Left to Tell: Discovering God Amidst the Rwandan Holocaust. (Carlsbad, CA: Hay House, 2006). Copyright © 2006 by Immaculée Ilibagiza. All rights reserved. Reprinted by permission of publisher.

Johnson, Jewell. The Top 100 Women of the Christian Faith. (Uhrichsville, OH: Barbour Publishers, 2009).

Jones, Mary Harris, with Edward F. Steele, editor. The Speeches and Writings of Mother Jones. (Pittsburgh, PA:Pittsburgh Press, 1988).

Kirvan, John, series editor. Let Nothing Disturb You: Teresa of Avila. (Notre Dame, IN: Ave Maria Press, 1996). Copyright © 1996, 2008 Quest Associates. All rights reserved. Used by permission of Ave Maria Press.

Klug, Lyn, editor. Soul Weavings: A Gathering of Women's Prayers.(Minneapolis, MN: Augsburg Fortress, 1996)

Krass, Peter. Sojourner Truth. (New York: Chelsea House, 1988).

Lee, Chana Kai. For Freedom's Sake: The Life of Fannie Lou Hamer. (Chicago: University of Illinois Press, 1999). Copyright 1999 by Board of Trustees of the University of Illinois. Used with permission of the University of Illinois Press.

Leonardo, Bianca and Winifred Rugg. Anne Hutchinson: Unsung Heroine of History. (Joshua Tree, CA: Tree of Life Publications, 1995).

Lutz, Lorry. Women as Risk-Takers for God. (Grand Rapids, MI: Baker Books, 1997).

Mackenzie, Catherine. Christian Heroines: Just Like Me and You? (Geanies House, Scotland: Christian Focus Publications, 2009).

Madigan, Shawn, C.S.J., editor. Mystics, Visionaries, & Prophets: A Historical Anthology of Women's Spiritual Writings. (Minneapolis, MN: Augsburg

Fortress Press, 1998). Copyright © 1998 Augsburg Fortress. All rights reserved. Used by permission of publisher.

"Mary Fisher, Christian Quaker, visiting the Ottoman Sultan Mehmet IV," in *Thoughts by Yursil*, December 3, 2008, at www.yursil.com.

Melille, Kelly & Annabell, editors. *Elizabeth Ann Seton: Selected Writings*. (New York: Paulist Press, 1987).

Mother Maria Skobtsova: Essential Writings. (Maryknoll, NY: Orbis Books, 2003).

Nuernberg, Leslie S. *Only Glory Awaits*. (Greenville, SC: Ambassador Emerald International, 2003).

O'Callaghan, Rosaria. *Flame of Love: A Biography of Nano Nagle* .(Milwaukee, WI: Bruce Press, 1960).

O'Farrell, Pius, and Hallidan, Therese. *Nano Nagle: A Story of Faith and Courage*. (Strasbourg, France: Sadifa Editions, 1983).

Osiek, Carolyn and Macdonald, Margaret Y. *A Woman's Place: House Churches in Earliest Christianity*. (Minneapolis, MN: Fortress Press, 2006).

Peers, Alison, Ed. *The Life of Saint Teresa of Avila*. (Garden City, NY: Image Books, 1960).

Pehanich, Very Rev. Edward. *Maria Skobtsova of Paris, Martyr of Ravensbrück*. (Johnstown, PA: The American Carpatho-Russian Orthodox Diocese of the U.S.A., www.acrod.org). © 2009 by The American Carpatho-Russian Orthodox Diocese of the U.S.A. All rights reserved. Used by permission.

Pettinger, T. "Joan of Arc Biography." (www.biographyonline.net, 2007.

Saint Teresa of Avila. *The Interior Castle* (NY: Crossroad Press, 1994).

Shewning, Walter, Ed. *Saints Are Not Sad*. F.J. Sheed (New York: Sheed & Ward Publishing, 1949).

Shore, Bill. *The Light of Conscience: How a Simple Act Can Change Your Life*. (New York: Random House, 2004).

Smith, T. Stratton *The Rebel Nun*. (Springfield, IL: Templegate Press, 1965).

Stanton, Sue. *Great Women of Faith: Inspiration for Action*. (Mahwah, NJ: Paulist Press, 2003).

Starkey, Marion L. *The Devil in Massachusetts*. (New York: Doubleday, 1969).

Starr, Mirabai, editor. *Saint Teresa of Avila*. (Boulder, CO: Sounds True, Inc., 2007). Copyright © 2007 Mirabai Starr. All rights reserved. Used by permission of Sounds True, Inc., Boulder, CO, www.SoundsTrue.com. .

Steele, Edward M., editor. *The Speeches and Writings of Mother Jones*. (Pittsburgh, PA: Pittsburgh Press, 1988).

Stjerna, Kirsi. *Women and the Reformation.* (Malden, MA: Blackwell Publishing, 2009)

Strachey, Lytton. *The Biography of Florence Nightingale.* (Blacksburg, VA: Wilder Publications, 2009).

Tapley, Charles Sutherland. *Rebecca Nurse: Saint but Witch Victim.*(Francetown, NH: Marshall Jones Publishers, 1995).

Ten Boom, Corrie. *Not I, But Christ.* (Grand Rapids, MI: Revell, a Division of Baker Books, 2000). Used with permission.

Ten Boom, Corrie; Buckingham, J. *Tramp for the Lord* (New York: Jove, 1974).

Ten Boom, Corrie, with Sherrill J., Sherrill S. *The Hiding Place.* (New York: Bantam, 1971)

Ten Boom, Corrie. *The Hiding Place.* (Grand Rapids, MI: Chosen Books, 1971).

Teresa of Avila. *The Interior Castle.* (Mahwah, NJ: Paulist Press, 1979).

"The Quakers: Hostile Bonnets and Gowns," at www.mayflowerfamilies. com/enquirer/quakers.htm.

"The Valiant Sixty: A Quaker's View," at www.westhillsfriends.org.

Tooley, Sarah A. *The Life of Florence Nightingale.* (Pratt Press, 2008)

Trask, Willard, translator and compiler. *Joan of Arc, in Her Own Words.* (New York: B•o•o•k•s & Co., A Turtle Point Imprint, 1996). Copyright © 1996. All rights reserved. Used by permission of publisher.

Truth, Sojourner (as dictated to Olive Gilbert). *Narrative of Sojourner Truth: A Bondswoman of Olden Time.* (Battle Creek, MI, 1878).

Tucker, Ruth A. and Liefeld, Walter, editors. *Daughters of the Church: Women and Ministry From New Testament Times to the Present.* (Grand Rapids, MI: Zondervan Publishing, 1987).

Walsh, Joseph J. *What Would You Die For? Perpetua's Passion.* (Baltimore, MD: Loyola College/Apprentice House, 2006). © 2006 by Loyola College in Maryland. All rights reserved. Used by permission of publisher.

Walsh, T. J. *Nano Nagle and the Presentation Sisters* (Dublin: M.H. Gill and Son Ltd., 1959). Copyright © M.H. Gill and Son Ltd., 1959. All rights reserved. Used by permission of Gill & Macmillan, publishers.

Warner, Marina. *Joan of Arc: The Image of Female Heroism.* (Berkeley and Los Angeles, CA: University of California Press, 1981).

Webb, Val. *Florence Nightingale: The Making of a Radical Theologian.* (St. Louis, MO: Chalice Press, 2002). Copyright © 2002 by Val Webb. All rights reserved. Used by permission of publisher via Copyright Clearance Center.

Williams, Joan. *Three Saints: Women Who Changed History.* (Skokie, IL: ACTA Publishing, 2006).

Williams, Selma R. Divine Rebel: The Life of Anne Marbury Hutchinson. (New York: Holt Rinehart & Winston, 1981).

About the Author

Marcy Heidish is an award-winning author of nine other books, including the acclaimed novel *A Woman Called Moses*, which was made into a television movie starring Cicely Tyson. In addition to *Defiant Daughters*, Heidish has published six novels and three nonfiction books, plus many short pieces.

She has also taught creative writing at Georgetown University, the George Washington University, and Fordham University.

In addition, she has been a committed volunteer in homeless shelters, a hospital, a hospice, a prison, on a hot line, and at the Lighthouse for the Blind. She also participates in a program that allows her to mentor recently incarcerated women.

Heidish is a Benedictine Oblate and a member of the Order of Saint Luke.